Beginning Craft, Design and Technology

Graphics and Design

R.W. Boycott and J. Bolan

Edward Arnold

© R.W. Boycott and J. Bolan 1985

First published in Great Britain 1985
by Edward Arnold (Publishers) Ltd
41 Bedford Square, London WC1B 3DQ

Edward Arnold (Australia) Pty Ltd
80 Waverley Road
Caulfield East
Victoria 3145
Australia

British Library Cataloguing in Publication Data

Boycott, R.W.
    Graphics and design.—(Beginning craft, design
    and technology)
    1. Commercial art
    I. Title   II. Bolan, J.   III. Series
    741.6   NC997

ISBN 0-7131-0978-5

Text set in 10/11 CRTronic 300 Univers
by The Castlefield Press, Moulton, Northampton
Printed in Great Britain
by Thomson Litho Ltd, East Kilbride, Scotland

Contents

Preface

The prime intention of this book is to stimulate interest and enjoyment in graphics and design among pupils of 11–14 years during their first, and in many cases only experience of craft, design and technology. The tasks suggested are simple in concept so that pupils should not meet with insuperable difficulties.

A specific aim of this book is to introduce the pupils to graphics and give them confidence in a society where so much information is presented in graphical form.

The book does not attempt to replace the teacher's individual approach to the subject; understandably, most teachers prefer their own method of introducing pupils to the techniques and equipment used in the graphics room. Material that students will be familiar with is used to illustrate a variety of techniques by which information can be communicated clearly and graphically. To help pupils, there is a short list of equipment needed to complete the work, at the beginning of each chapter.

The design techniques explained in this book are intended to develop creative thinking as well as visual awareness. Pupils are introduced to a logical system of design which will help them to identify and solve simple problems. Further, the authors emphasise the desirability of linking designs prepared in the graphics course with projects made in the workshops.

The assignments and examples used in this book can be readily modified or developed further to cover varying needs in different schools.

All dimensions are in millimetres (mm) unless otherwise indicated.

Acknowledgements

Many people in education and industry have given their help in the preparation of this book. Bob White and Geoff Sharples have given their time generously, and we are indebted to Kath Webster for her faultless typing. The ideas in the book came from many sources, and the authors wish to thank all the pupils and teachers who have helped, especially Terry Wiggett and Ron Underdown who gave every encouragement and support. Finally, without the patience and understanding of our wives and families, the writing of this book would not have been possible.

Permissions

The publishers would like to thank Esso Petroleum Co. Ltd. for permission to reproduce the diagrams on p 14 which are reprinted from *Esso Oilways International* vol. 29, No 1 c 1983.

1 Fun with lines

A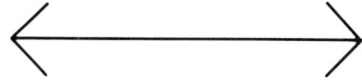

B

Lines can be fun.

Look at the lines **A, B, C** and **D** opposite. They are all different lengths – or are they?

C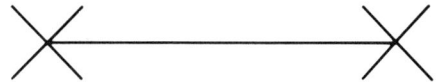

Measure them with a rule and find out.

The diagrams below are made from lines.

D

E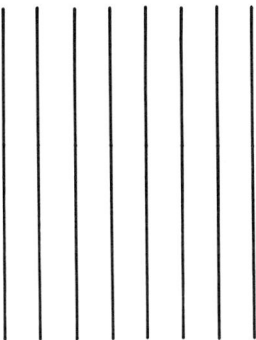

F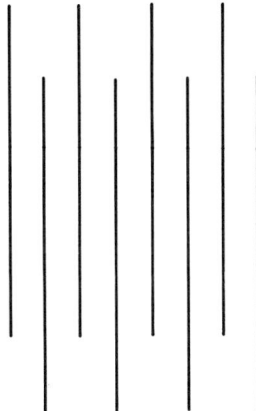

G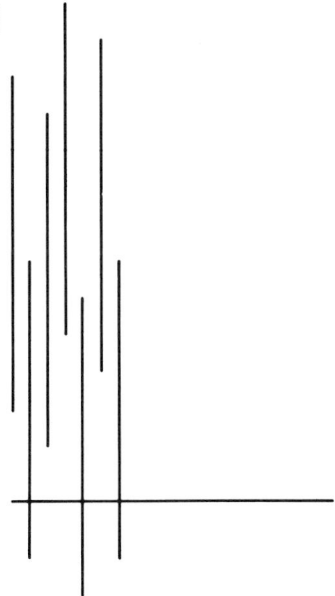

E, F and **G** are made up of eight lines of equal length.

E and **F** are made up entirely from vertical lines, but **G** includes one horizontal line.

Which diagram is the most interesting?

Things To Do

1. Using ten vertical lines all 50 mm long, experiment with various arrangements to produce the most interesting design.

2. Repeat question **1**, but this time add horizontal lines to your design.

5

Lines can be different thicknesses. You can find a pattern of lines like those opposite on many different products in shops. (Look at the back cover of this book.) These lines can be 'read' by a scanning laser-beam and help the shopkeeper keep control of his stock.

Experiment with lines of different thicknesses to produce the most interesting pattern.

Many electronic instruments, watches, calculators, etc. have digital LCD or LED displays. The diagram below shows such a display and how a figure is generated on the linear grid.

What do the initials LCD and LED stand for?

000403001590

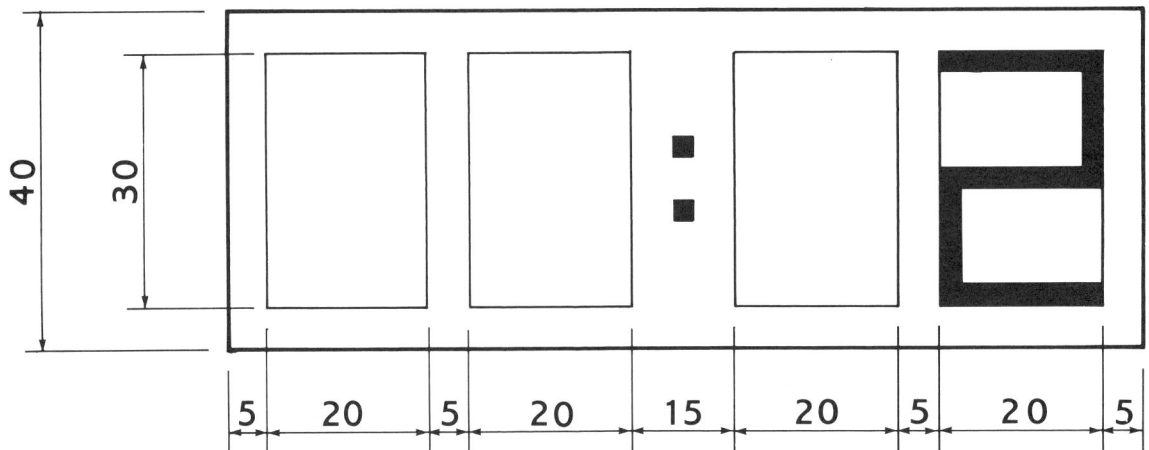

Things To Do

Construct several grids like the one shown above. Thicken the lines on the grid to show:

1. The time your favourite TV programme starts.

2. The time you leave home on a normal school day.

3. 1 hour and 50 minutes after midday.

4. 33 minutes after midnight.

6

Many electronic calculators use an LCD display of eight characters. These displays are supposed to show numbers only, but with a little imagination they can be made to show letters as well.

Opposite are shown the letters which can be generated on such a display. The letter S for example, is the number 5 when viewed upside down.

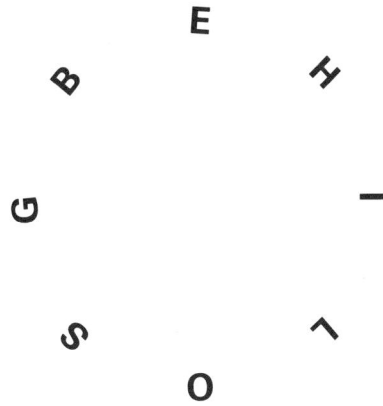

E

B   H

G   —

S   ^

O

The number 71077345 above becomes completely different if viewed from the other way round. Turn this page upside down to read the hidden word.

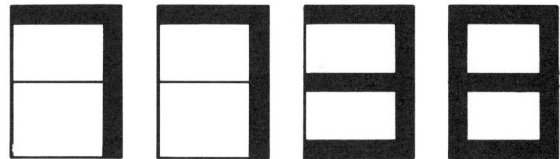

Many words can be made this way. Not all the eight numbers need be used.

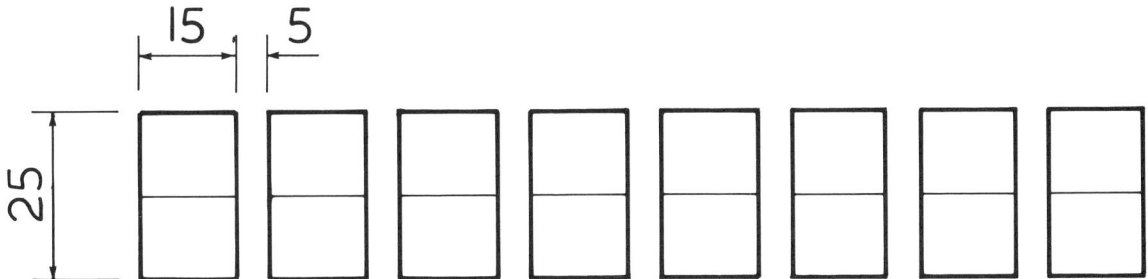

15   5

25

Things To Do

Draw grids, like the one above and make up the words, using numbers only. Remember, to read the word in numbers **1** and **2**, you will have to turn the finished grid upside down.

1. A greeting – 07734

2. Footwear – 53045

In numbers **3** to **5**, work out the word and draw it on the grid.

3. Distress signal – ? *(3 letters)*

4. Grain Store – ? *(4 letters)*

5. Favourite pastimes – ? *(7 letters)*

6. Draw several grids and see how many words you can make using numbers.

7

Can you recognise the following shapes? They are all made from straight horizontal and vertical lines on a 5 mm square grid.

Is this a cowboy or a Mexican frying an omelette?

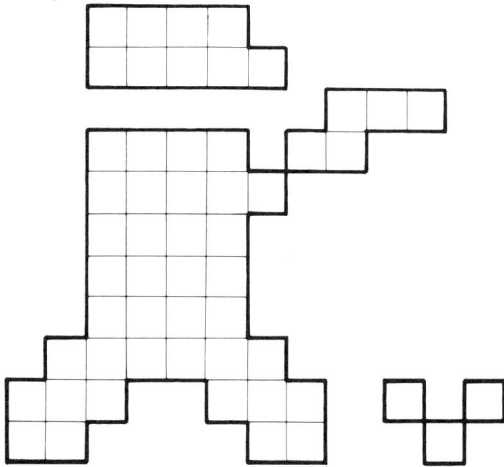

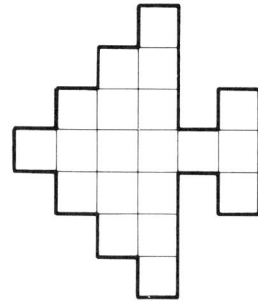

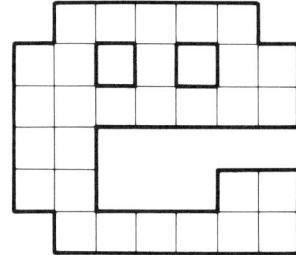

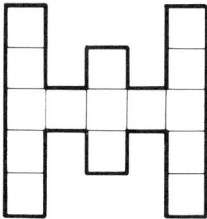

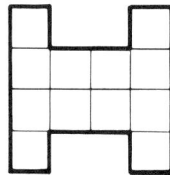

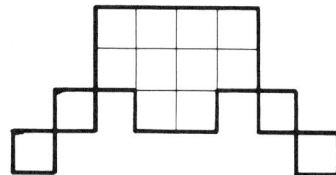

Things To Do

On 5 mm squared paper, draw:

1. An alien spaceship

2. A friendly robot

3. Your home space-port

4. A fire-breathing monster

5. A submarine

6. A laser-cannon

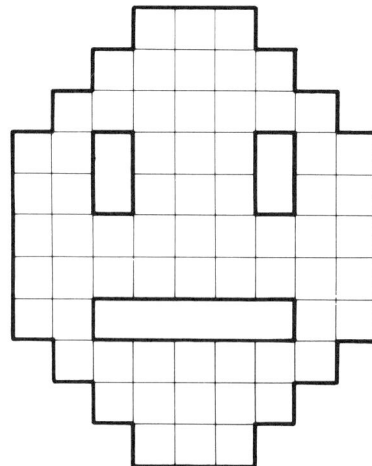

2 Showing information

Bar Charts

A bar chart is a simple and quick way of comparing things. It is drawn with vertical and horizontal lines and can be made clearer by using colour.

The bar chart below shows the frequency (the number of times) each letter appears in the tongue-twister – *She sells sea shells on the sea shore*. You can see that the letter **s** for example occurs twice as many times as the letter **h**.

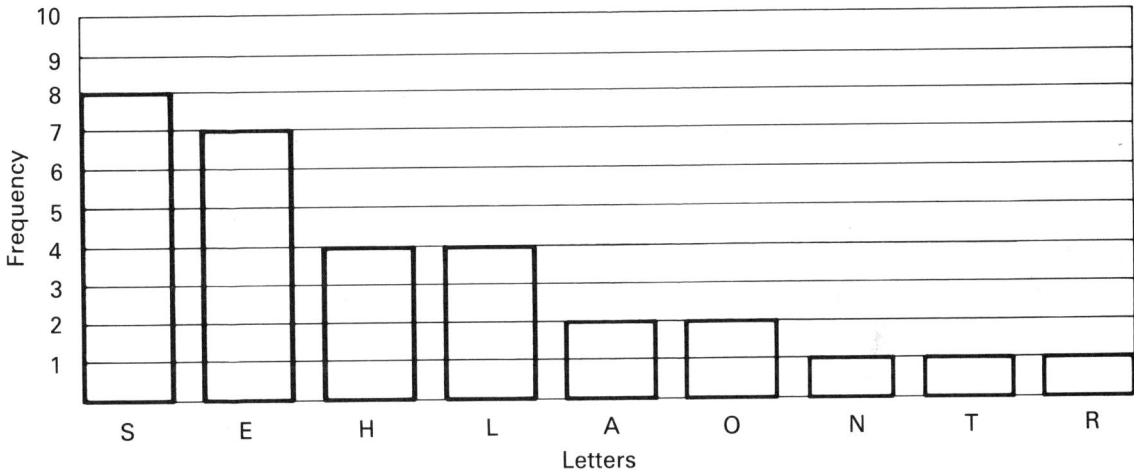

Things To Do

1. Draw a bar chart to show the frequency that each letter appears in:

   (a) Peter Piper picked a peck of pickled peppers.
   (b) Round the rugged rock the ragged rascal ran.

2. Make a list of the names of 25 pop stars or footballers. Draw a bar chart to show the frequency of the first letters of their last names e.g. Fred Bear – B is the first letter of the last name.

Find out the following information and then draw a bar chart:

3. How many people in your class travel to school in the morning by each of the following methods?

   (a) walking
   (b) bus
   (c) car
   (d) bicycle
   (e) train
   (f) other

4. How many pupils in your class have birthdays in the different months of the year?

Graphs

Graphs are another useful way of presenting information. They show how something alters over a given period of time. All graphs must have a horizontal and vertical axis both clearly labelled to show the information which is being presented e.g. months of the year, amount of produce sold, etc.

The graph opposite shows the volume of sun-tan lotion sales. You can see the increase in sales as the summer approaches and then a dramatic decline after August. Why is this so?

The graph below shows how many boys and girls are out of school on trips and visits between Monday and Saturday. The greatest number, 35, occurs on Saturday. Why do you think this is so? What was the total number of pupils out of school during the week?

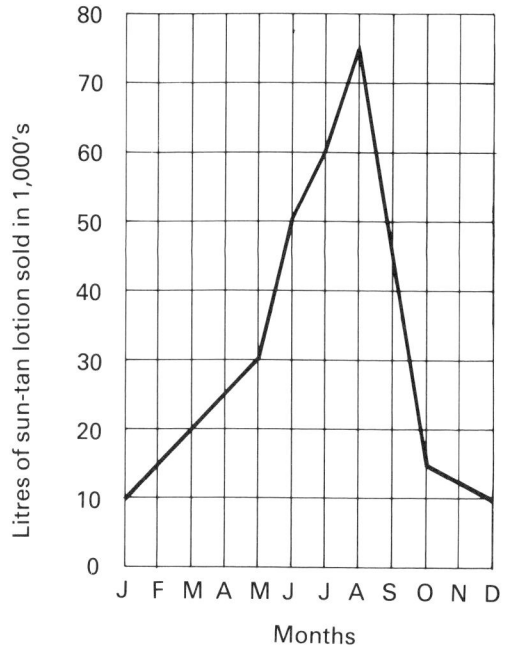

Things To Do

1. This list show the number of bottles of perfume sold by a shop over one year:

Jan – 10	Feb – 12	Mar – 11
Apr – 13	May – 15	Jun – 16
Jul – 16	Aug – 15	Sep – 16
Oct – 18	Nov – 21	Dec – 37

   Draw a graph to show how the sales vary over the year. Why do you think there is an increase in sales in December?

2. The average temperatures for each month, in degrees Celsius, are recorded below:

Jan – 6	Feb – 7	Mar – 10
Apr – 13	May – 16	Jun – 19
Jul – 22	Aug – 22	Sep – 18
Oct – 14	Nov – 10	Dec – 7

   Draw a graph to show this information.

3. A garage which opens for ten hours a day sells petrol at the rates shown below:

   8 a.m. to 9 a.m. – 200 litres
   9 a.m. to 10 a.m. – 75 litres
   10 a.m. to 11 a.m. – 100 litres
   11 a.m. to 12 noon – 150 litres

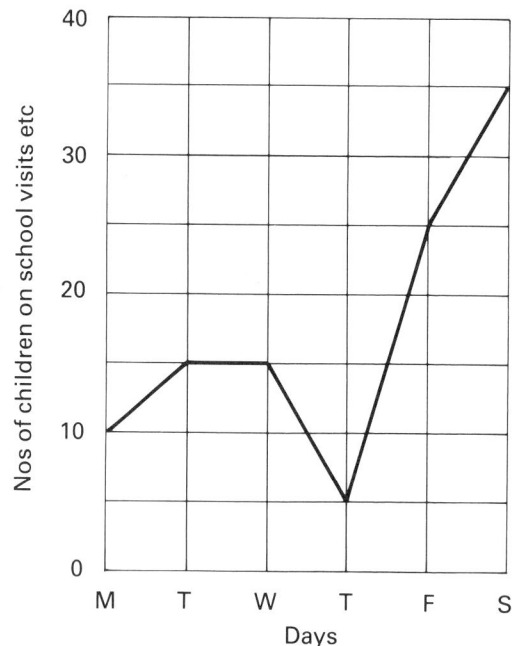

   12 noon to 1 p.m. – 250 litres
   1 p.m. to 2 p.m. – 300 litres
   2 p.m. to 3 p.m. – 150 litres
   3 p.m. to 4 p.m. – 200 litres
   4 p.m. to 5 p.m. – 300 litres
   5 p.m. to 6 p.m. – 450 litres

   Draw a graph to show how the sales vary throughout the day.

Pie Charts

Pie charts give us information in an easy-to-read form showing the way items are shared out. They look like pies divided into slices, each slice representing a proportion or percentage of the whole pie.

The circle represents the sum of all the information (data) available. As a circle contains 360° (degrees), one quarter (25%) of the data equals 90° of the circle. Therefore 1% of the data = 3.6°.

Study chart **A** opposite. This shows how a family divided an apple pie. Jayne had a quarter (25%), Geoff also had a quarter and Lynne who was hungry ate the rest.

In a school of 100 pupils, 50 stay for school meals, 40 go home and 10 buy their food from a local sandwich shop. Pie chart **B** shows how this information can be presented.

Chart **C** shows approximately, how the government planned to spend the nation's money in 1983/84.

Things To Do

Draw pie charts to show:

1. How your TV viewing time is divided between the four major channels on one day of the week.

2. The expenditure of a family who spend £150 per month on rent, £100 on food, £50 on entertainment, and £50 on all other items.

3. The hair-colour grouping of pupils in your class, using the following categories:

   (a) light   (blonde/light brown)
   (b) dark   (black/dark brown)
   (c) other   (ginger, etc)

   You may include your teacher in the sample. If he or she is bald, count them in the light category.

A

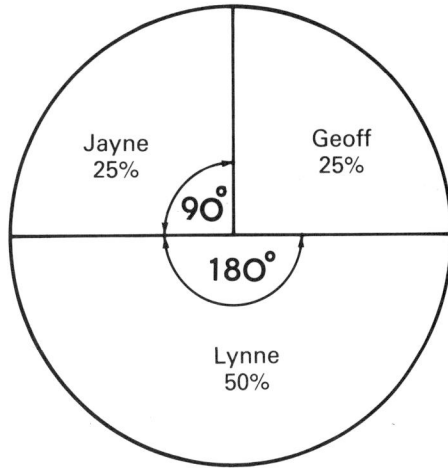

B

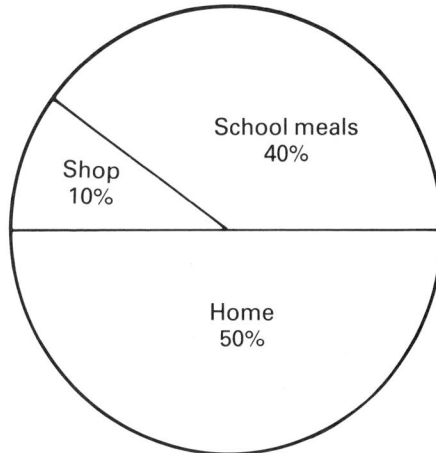

C

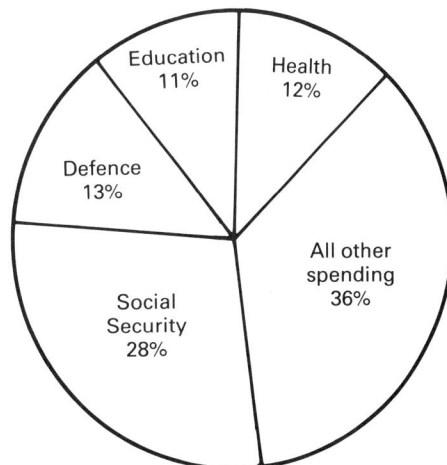

Flow Charts

Flow charts show step by step instructions for making or doing something. They give us a clear picture of how certain things can be done. Again colour can be used to make them look more attractive.

Flow chart **A** opposite shows the stages in unlocking a door.

Flow chart **B** shows the first stages of filling an electric kettle to make a cup of tea. Copy the given information and then complete the chart in as many stages as you think necessary, to make a cup of tea.

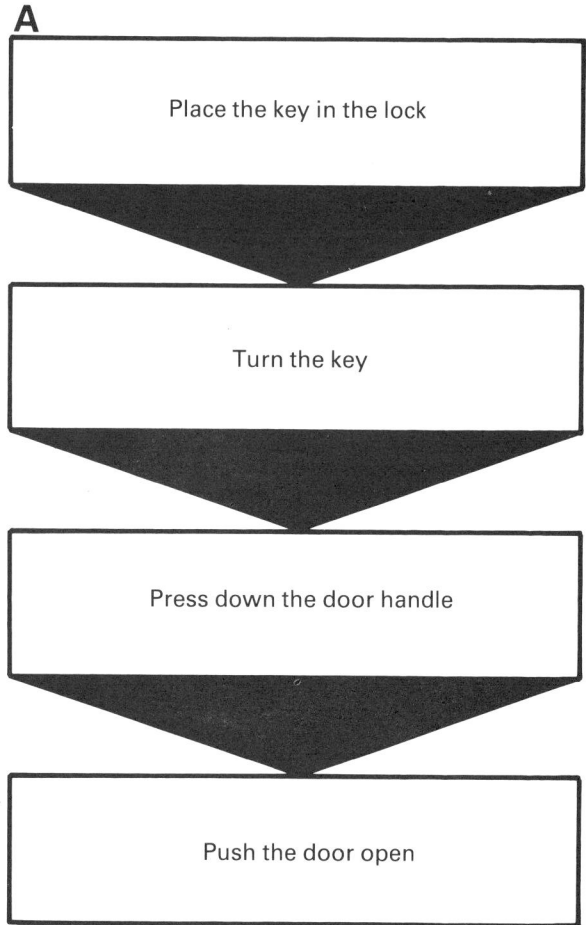

A

Place the key in the lock

Turn the key

Press down the door handle

Push the door open

B

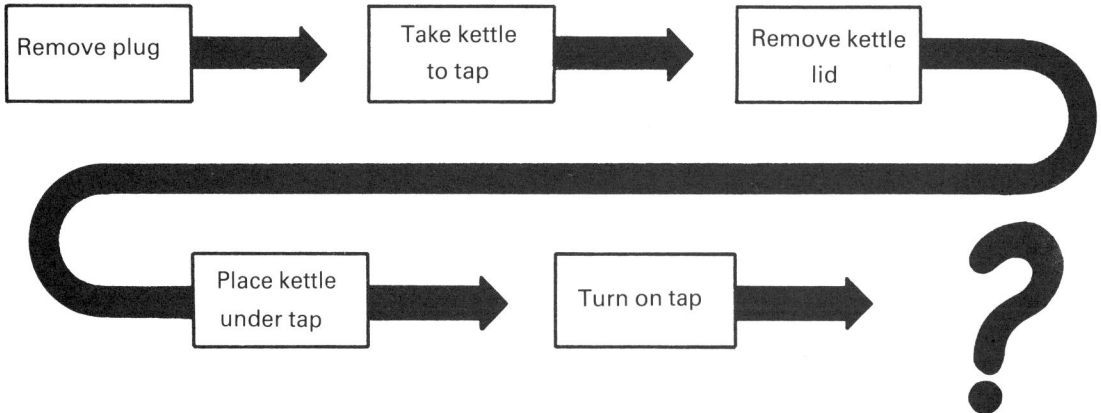

Remove plug → Take kettle to tap → Remove kettle lid → Place kettle under tap → Turn on tap → ?

Things To Do

Design and draw your own flow charts to show how to:

1. Tune your radio into your favourite station.

2. Insert a cassette tape into a cassette player.

3. Make a piece of toast.

4. Clean a bicycle.

5. Set a table for a meal.

12

3 Symbols

Symbols are used in everyday life to give information in a visual form. Road signs and company logos are common examples of the use of symbols.

Below are symbols which represent four types of transport. Can you name them?

The symbol opposite is made from circles and rectangles. What does it represent?

Things To Do

You are going to invent some symbols of your own. In the box below are some points you should consider when thinking about your designs.

Boxes like this appear throughout the book. They will remind you of what to think about when designing something.

Design Considerations

(a) Simple shapes are best.
(b) Clear layouts have most visual impact.

Design symbols for six of the following. Your symbols can be drawn on black card, cut out and glued onto white paper.

1. A taxi firm
2. A swimming club
3. An orchestra
4. A rounders team
5. A zoo
6. A travel agency
7. A playground
8. A car-park
9. A chess club
10. A discotheque
11. A cricket club
12. A ballet school

A person driving a car needs to have information about the car's overall performance at a glance.

Above is an example of a high-technology dashboard display. Some new cars use a solid-state LCD, to provide the driver with an information centre that monitors the car's basic functions.

What do the 5 symbols on this dashboard display mean?

Things To Do

You are going to design your own driver information centre.

> **Design Considerations**
> (a) The display must be clear.
> (b) Clear symbols will be easy to recognise.
> (c) The layout must be simple.

1. Design a vehicle dashboard display to show:

   (a) engine rpm
   (b) fuel state
   (c) oil pressure
   (d) mpg
   (e) speed

Below is a vehicle map which would alert the driver to many potential problems inside the car.

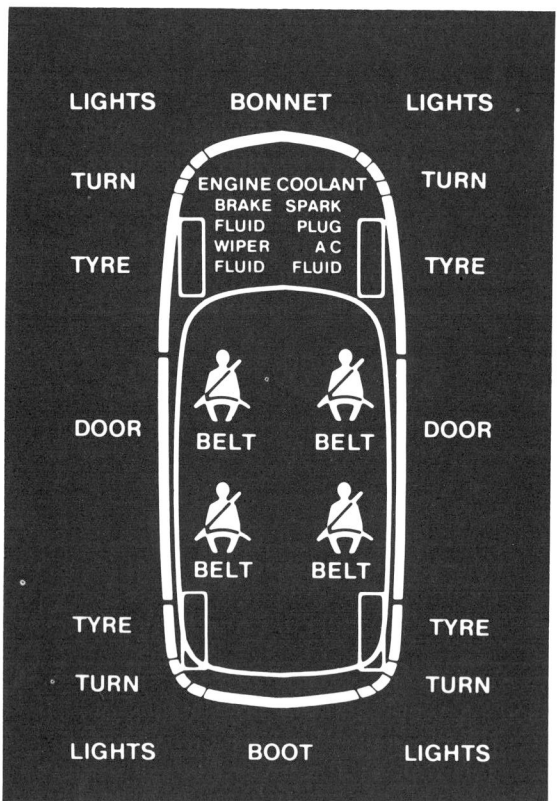

2. Design a vehicle map to warn of problems with:

   (a) tyres
   (b) brakes
   (c) lights
   (d) doors

Below is a map of part of the British Isles drawn by a computer.

Can you name the three cities and river shown on this map?

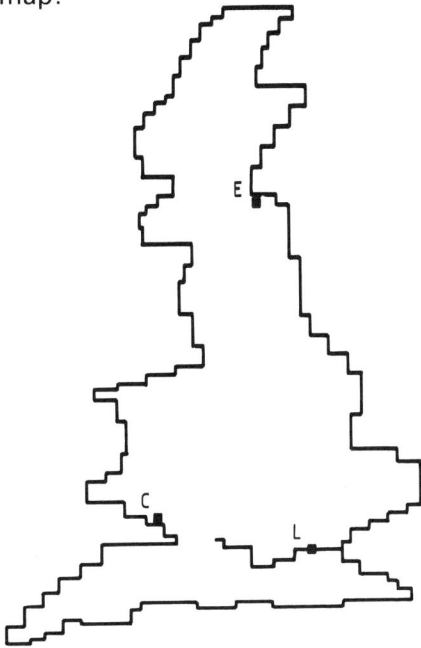

To interpret a map you need a **key** like the one below. Symbols, like these, show the main features of a map,

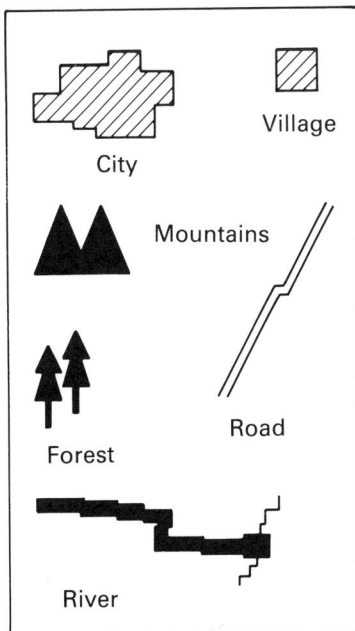

City

Village

Mountains

Forest

Road

River

Weather symbols are familiar to most of us. Below are some examples.

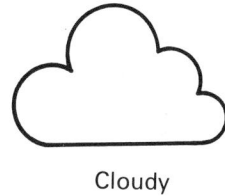

Sunny

Cloudy and wet

FOG

Lightning

Cloudy

Things To Do

1. Design weather symbols of your own to represent:

    (a) snow
    (b) ice
    (c) hail
    (d) storm
    (e) wind

2. Imagine an island in a vast ocean. Draw a computer plan of your island and mark on it any major features. Invent symbols of your own and produce a key to explain them.

3. What would the weather be like on your island, during a typical day in:

    (a) spring
    (b) summer
    (c) autumn
    (d) winter

    Draw only the outline of the island, and position weather symbols on it to show a typical day in spring, summer, autumn and winter. If you wish cut your symbols from coloured card.

15

4 Scale drawing

Sometimes to draw an object full or life-size would be impossible; for example a large dinosaur or a very tiny micro-chip. A scale drawing allows such objects to be drawn to a convenient size while showing their correct proportions.

A drawing is **scaled up** if it is drawn larger than life-size; for example the drawing of a micro-chip will be many times bigger than the actual size.

A drawing is **scaled down** when it is smaller than full-size; for example the plans of a building will be many times smaller than the actual size.

A Original

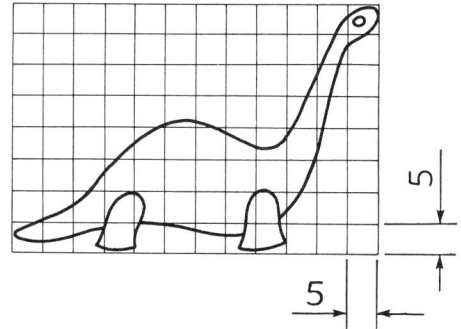

Study drawing **A** of Dyllis the Dinosaur shown above.

If we reproduce the grid that has been drawn around the dinosaur, but increase the size of the squares, we can enlarge the drawing as in **B** below. Notice how the proportions remain unaltered. Dyllis below is **twice** as big as Dyllis above.

B 2:1 of original

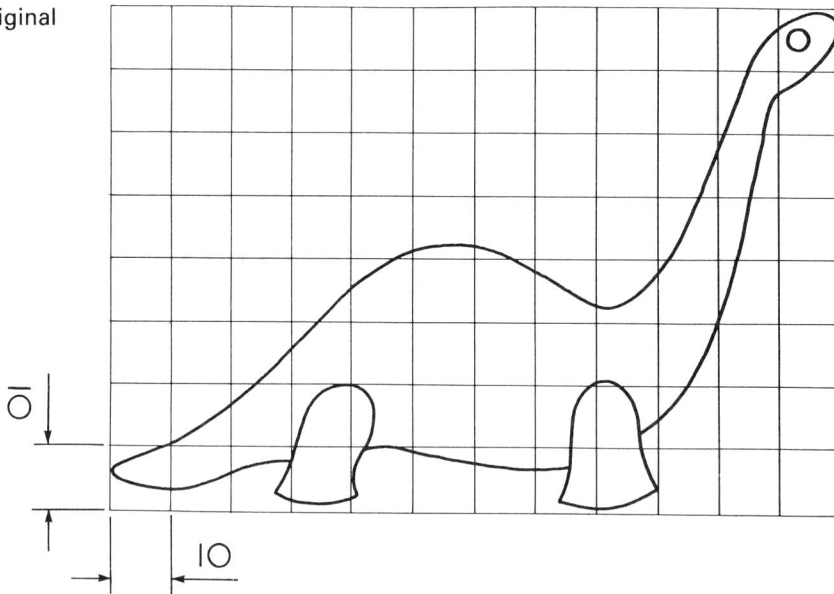

C Scale 1:1

D Scale 2:1

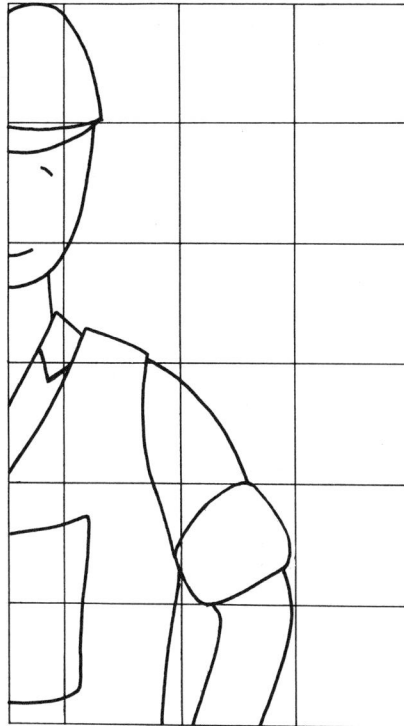

E

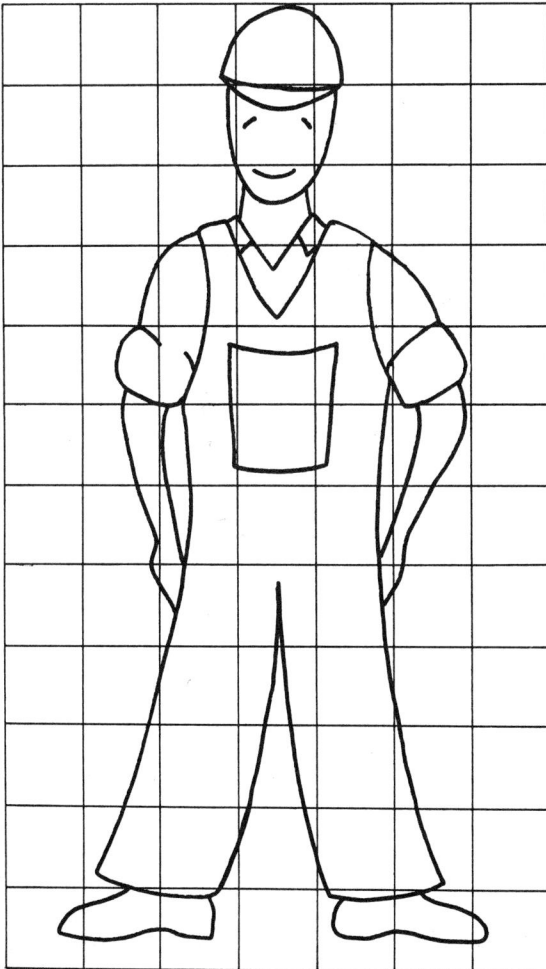

Here are sketches of a cartoon character within a square grid. Drawing **C** is the first or original drawing at a scale of 1:1. In drawing **D** the size of the squares has been doubled and thus the character is twice the scale of the original, at a scale of 2:1.

This method can be useful to enlarge or reduce just a particular part of a drawing as in **E** above.

Things To Do

1. Inside a grid with squares measuring 8 × 8 mm draw Dyllis's cousin Denis the dinosaur.

2. Draw or sketch several ideas for characters to appear on a safety poster. These originals need only be about 60 mm high. Scale up your best idea so that it will be suitable for a poster measuring 240 × 120 mm.

3. Enlarge either part of one of your drawings, or part of one of the above drawings.

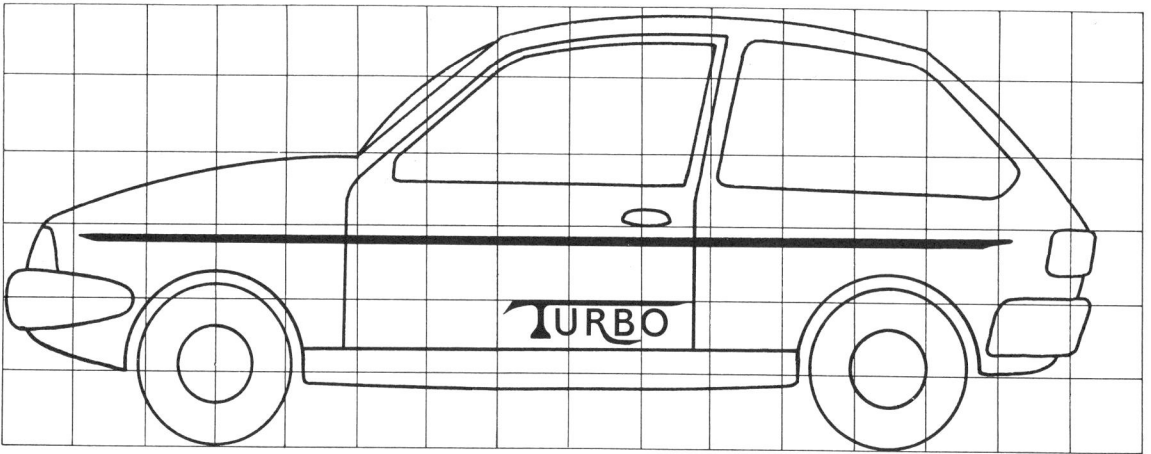

A motor car

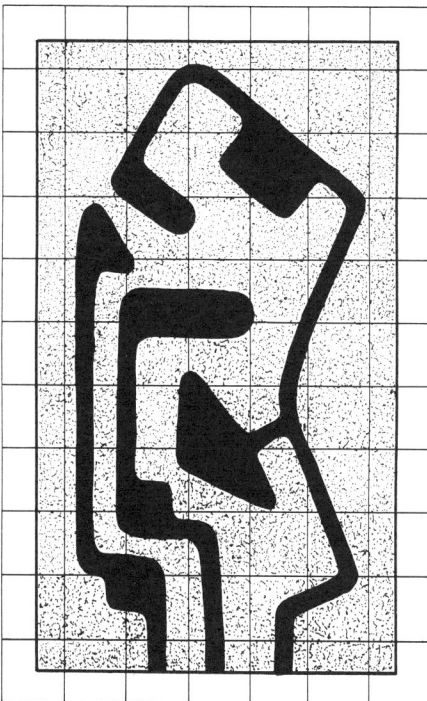

A Printed Circuit Board (PCB)

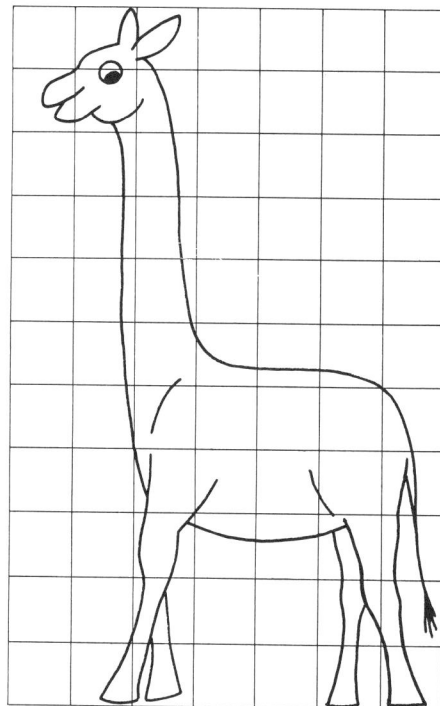

A friendly llama

Things To Do

The PCB and llama above are drawn inside a grid. Each square in the grid represents a 10 mm square. Redraw:

1. The PCB so that it is twice the above size (scale 2 : 1).

2. The llama so that it is twice the size shown above.

The car is drawn inside a 10 mm square grid.

3. Draw the motor car so that it is within a grid with squares measuring 8 × 8 mm.

4. Copy the grid only from the motor car drawn above. Design a motor car of your own within this grid and then enlarge it to twice that size.

Drawings made up of horizontal and vertical lines can be easily scaled without the help of a grid.

The floor plan of a room is shown on the right. It has been drawn to a scale of 1:100 which means that 1 mm on this plan represents 100 mm in the actual room.

A plan shows a bird's-eye view of something.

Things To Do

1. Redraw the plan of the room to a scale of 1:50.

2. Calculate the minimum number of carpet tiles one metre square that are required to completely cover the floor.

3. These carpet tiles are available in different colours. Work out an interesting pattern (use the same scale as in **1.**) to cover the floor.

4. Below is an outline plan (a bird's-eye view) of a school building. It is drawn to a scale of 1:1000. Redraw the school plan to a scale of:

(a) 1:500
(b) 1:1500

Learnalot Comprehensive Scale 1:1000

Dimensions in metres

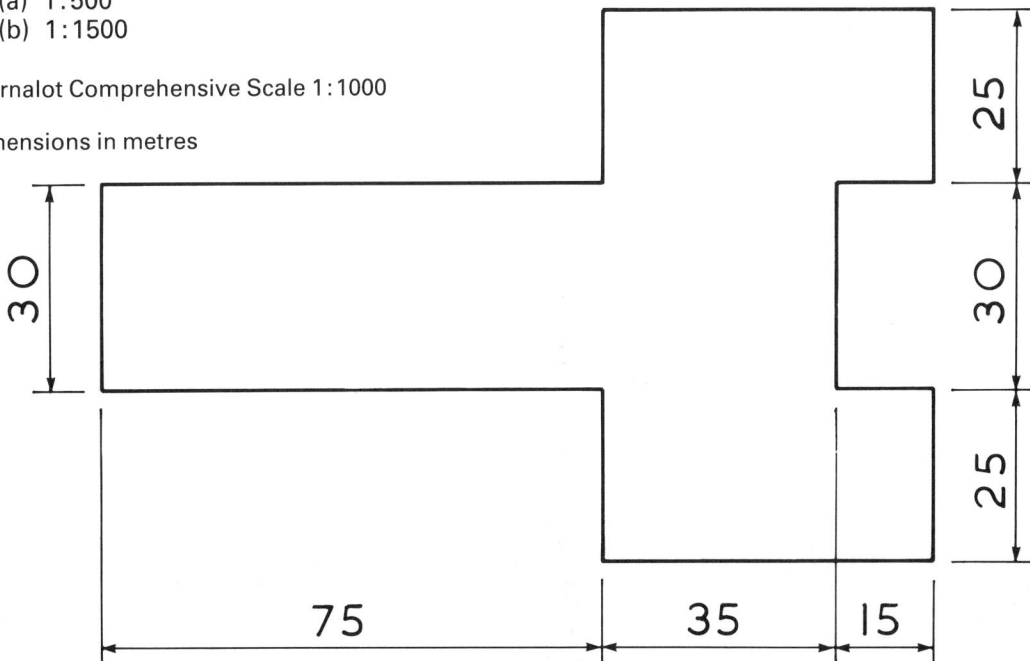

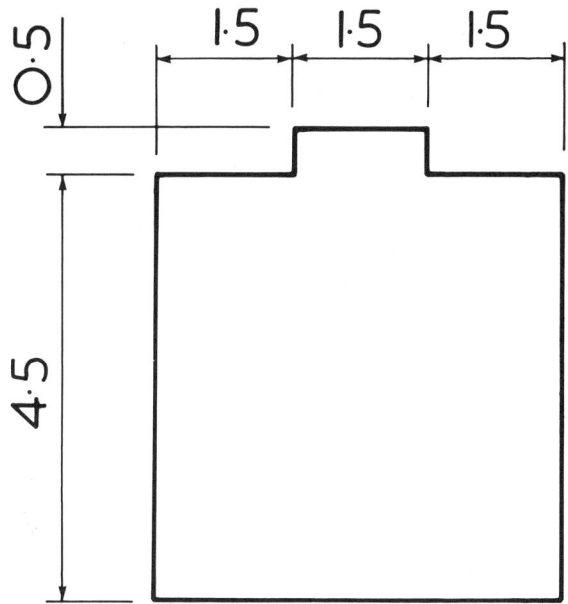

Dimensions in metres

5 Plans

A plan shows what something looks like from above. For example a road map is a plan of a road system. It shows how the roads would appear from an aeroplane.

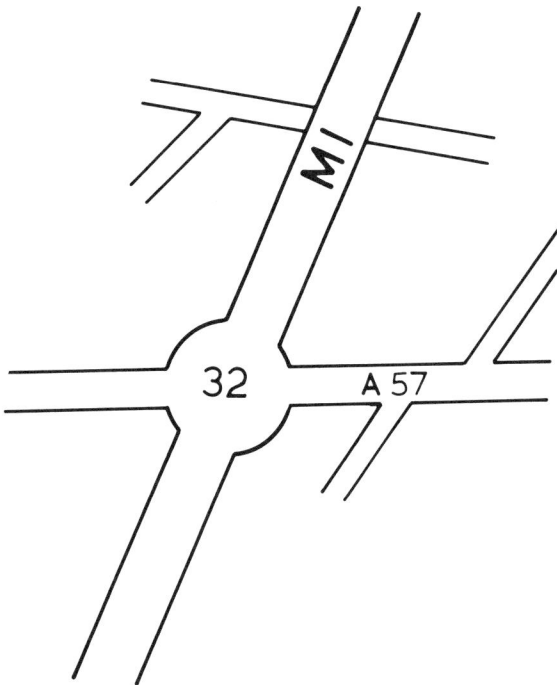

The plan of the classroom below is drawn to a scale of 1:100. This means that every mm of the plan is equal to 100 mm in actual size.

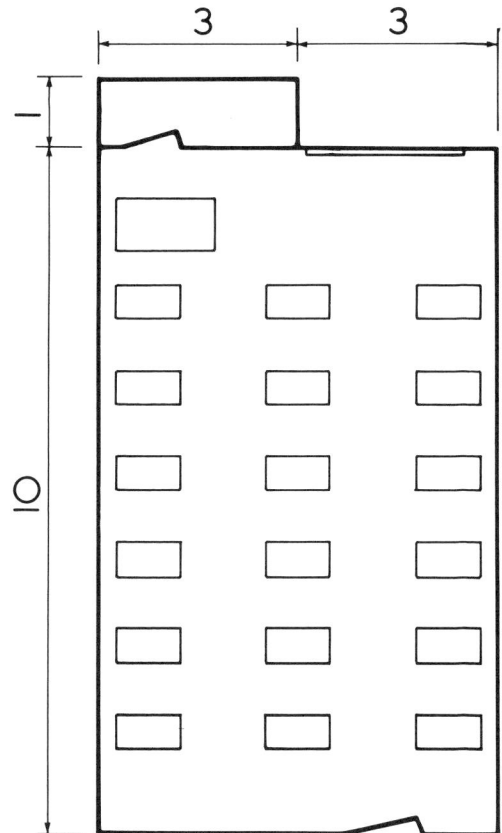

Dimensions in metres

As we have seen before, it is sometimes impractical to draw plans full or life-size. So they must be drawn to scale. This allows us to draw to a convenient size while maintaining the correct shape and proportion.

Things To Do

1. Draw a plan of your school and its grounds. Estimate the size and scale but try to keep your plan in correct proportion.

2. Draw free hand, a map to direct someone from school to your home.

3. Draw an approximate plan of one of the rooms in your house showing the position of the furniture.

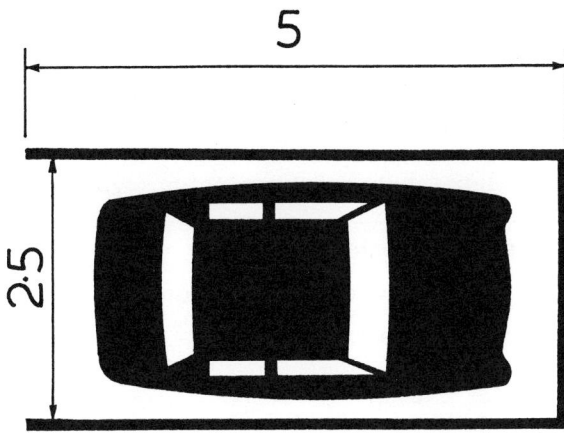

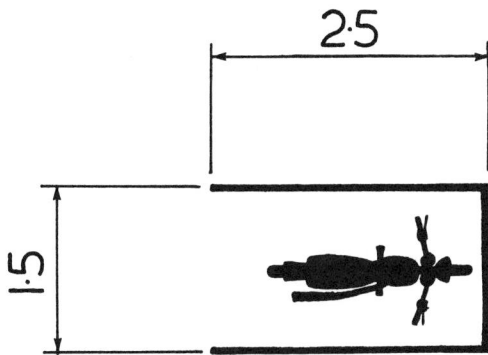

Dimensions in metres

The above plans show a car and motor bike in parking spaces.

On the right, drawn to a different scale, is a plan of the land available for a car-park.

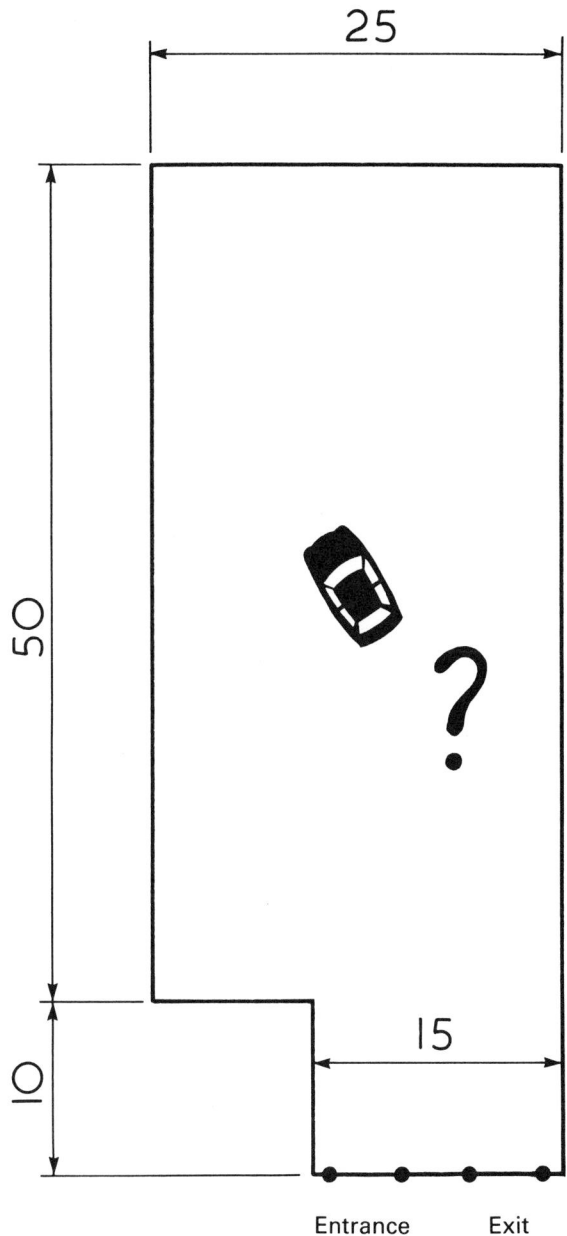

Things To Do

Draw a scale plan of the above car-park with your design for the arrangement of parking spaces.

It might help if you draw your plan of the car-park to a scale of 1 : 250 and then cut out pieces of card, to the same scale, to represent the areas required by individual cars and motor bikes. By moving your pieces of card into various positions, you will be able to select the arrangement you think best.

Design Considerations

(a) The entrance and exit points must be kept clear.
(b) Cars need room to manoeuvre.
(c) Do not allow cars to be blocked in.
(d) Try to make the best use of the space available keeping in mind points (a), (b) and (c) above.

The outline plan of a desk top calculator is shown below with the position of the LCD display panel indicated. However, the operating keys are not shown.

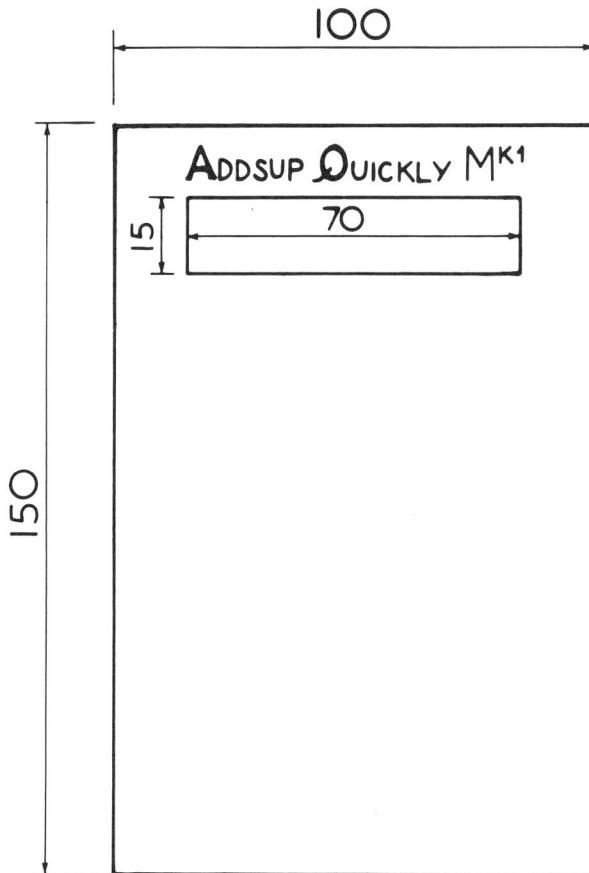

ADDSUP QUICKLY M^{K1}

70

15

100

150

Why are display panels usually positioned above the keys on calculators?

Why is it important to have numbers and symbols on calculating keys which can be recognised in different countries?

The operating keys for the calculator drawn above are 10 × 10 mm.

Things To Do

1. Draw a full-size plan of the calculator shown opposite.

2. Design a suitable layout for the keyboard.

Design Considerations

(a) The following keys are required:

    1. Numbers 0 to 9
    2. $+ - \times \div \% =$
    3. C (clear)
    4. M (memory)
    5. ON/OFF
    6. Any others you think necessary.

(b) The keys should be spaced neatly on the key board.

(c) The keys should be grouped in a logical way.

---

3. Design a company logo suitable for use on the above calculator.

4. Hand-held computer games are very popular. Design and draw a full-size plan of a hand-held computer game which uses an LCD display to show what is happening. The overall size of your plan should be 150 × 80 mm and the display panel 70 × 70 mm. The keys should be 10 × 10 mm. Choose a theme for your game e.g. castles, knights, vampires or gremlins.

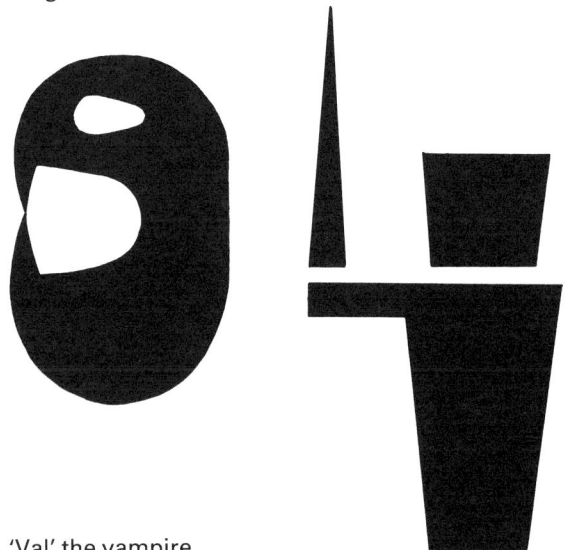

'Val' the vampire

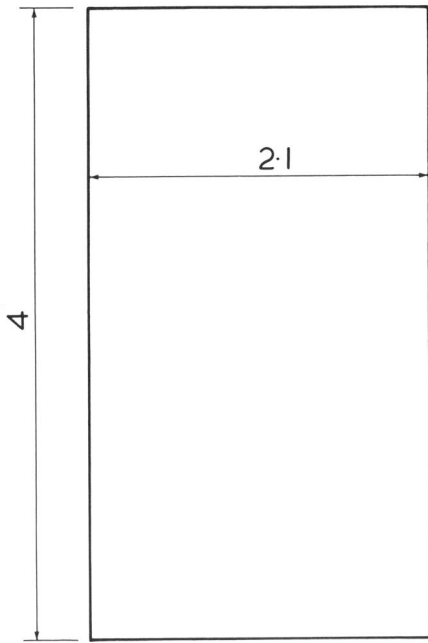

Dimensions in metres

The caravan will contain the following items which are drawn to a scale of 1:33.

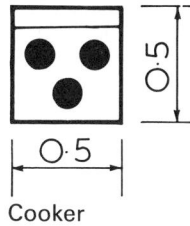

Cooker

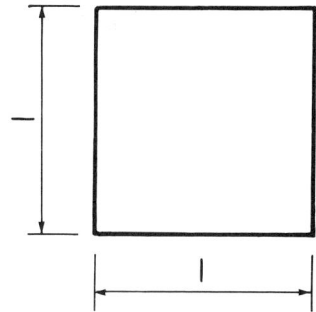

Table

The floor plan of a caravan is shown above, drawn to the scale of 1:50.

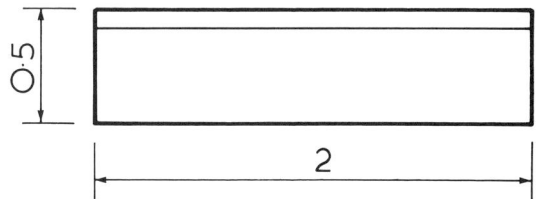

Seats

Things To Do

1. Draw an outline plan of the caravan above and show the positions of the door and windows.

2. Using pieces of card, cut to size to represent the furniture, make three different arrangements suitable for a two-berth caravan.

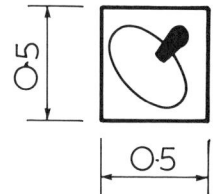

Sink

Design Considerations

(a) The floor space should not be too cluttered.
(b) The furniture should be arranged in a logical way.
(c) A separate bedroom? If so an interior wall and door may be needed.

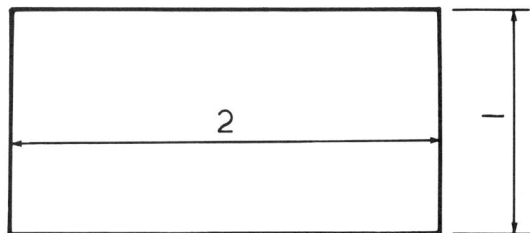

Bed

3. Choose the most comfortable arrangement of furniture for your caravan and draw it to the same scale as above.

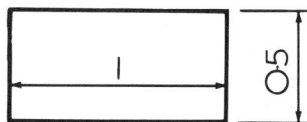

Wardrobe

Dimensions in metres

6 Pictorial views – perspective and isometric

There are many types of pictorial drawing (drawings that look like a picture). This chapter deals with two; perspective and isometric. Both give a three-dimensional view of an object.

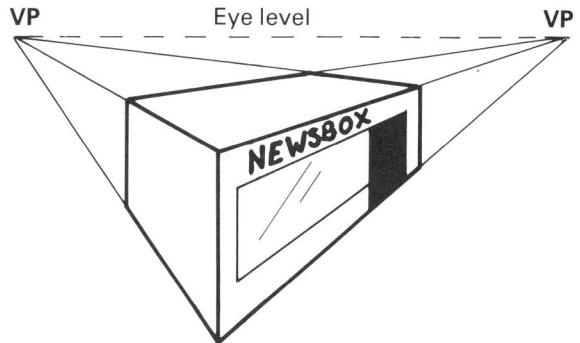

The drawing above shows the outline of a single shop building.

Perspective Views

Perspective drawing, the type we will look at first, gives us an idea of how the object will actually look.

The further away from us an object is, the smaller it looks. The sun is many times larger than the moon but because it is further away from the earth it looks only slightly larger.

Below is a drawing of a row of such shops. If the row were long enough the shops would seem to vanish into the distance.

The point where the buildings appear to vanish is called the **vanishing point**.

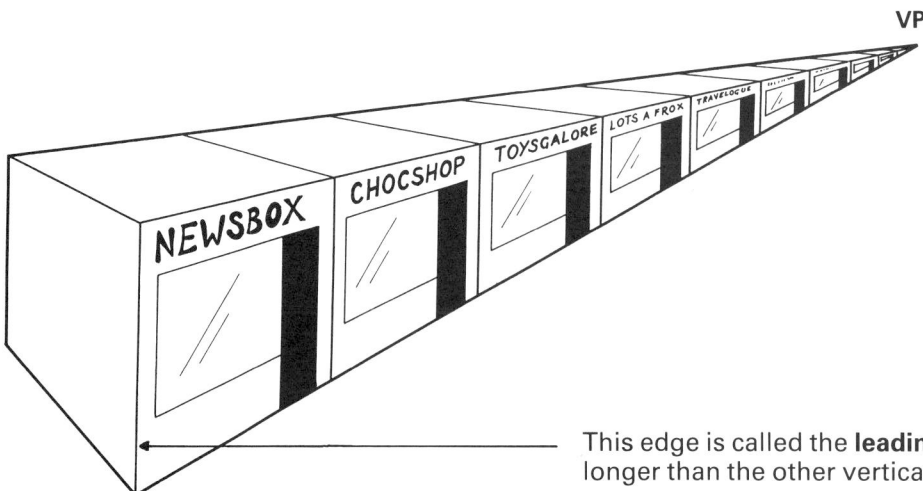

This edge is called the **leading edge**. Why is it longer than the other vertical edges?

How to draw a Perspective View

1. Draw the leading edge and position the vanishing point **VP1**.

2. Connect the leading edge to **VP1** and complete the drawing.

·
VP1

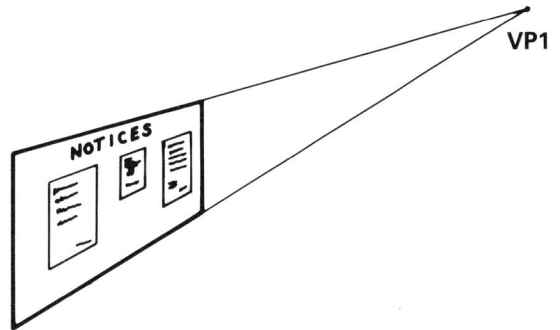

Sometimes two vanishing points may be needed.

1. Draw the leading edge, and position the vanishing points **VP1** and **VP2**. Connect these to the leading edge.

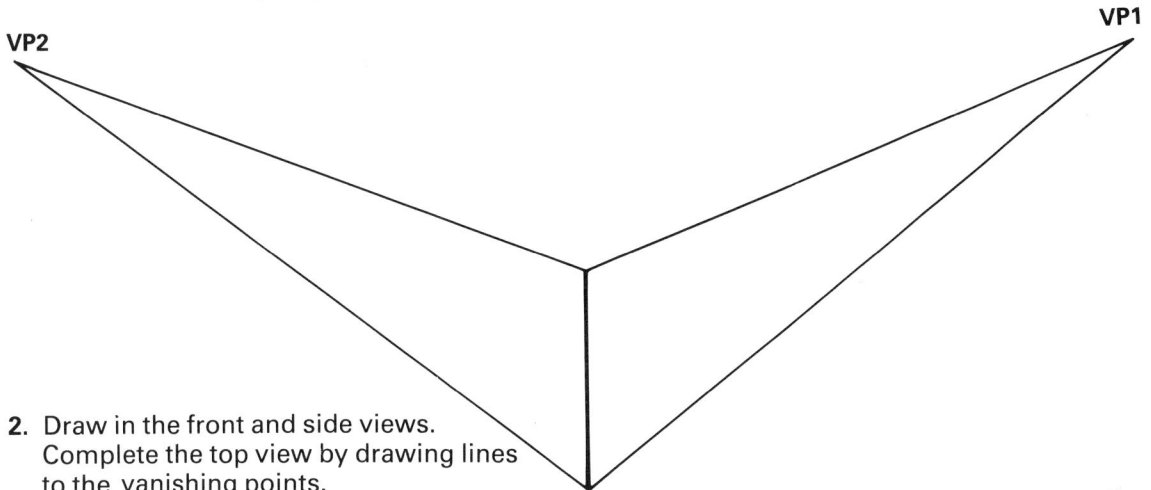

2. Draw in the front and side views. Complete the top view by drawing lines to the vanishing points.

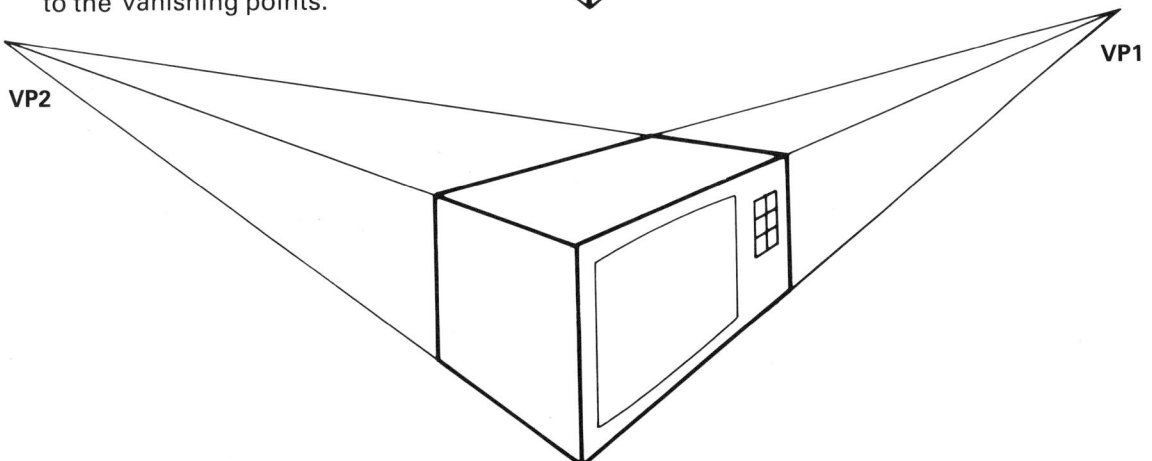

Things To Do

1. The front and end views of a matchbox are shown opposite. Redraw this box so that it is shown as a perspective view.

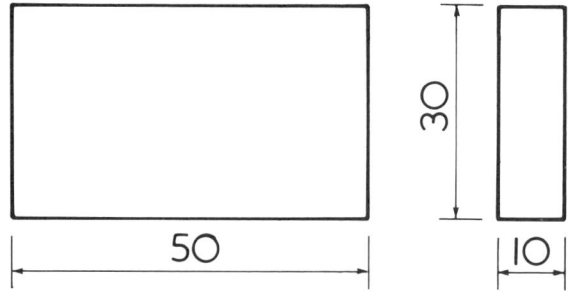

2. One face of a fascinating mathematical puzzle is shown opposite. This is the Rubic cube, named after its inventor, Professor Erno Rubic. Each face of the cube is made up of nine smaller faces which can be one of six different colours.

   Draw the cube in perspective. You may colour the faces if you wish with coloured pencils.

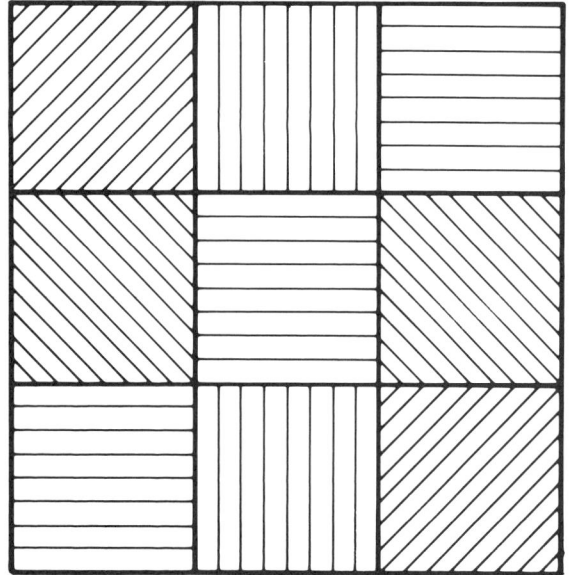

3. Below is the plan view of part of an airfield runway. Draw the view of the runway that you would see as a pilot in the cockpit of an aeroplane coming in to land.

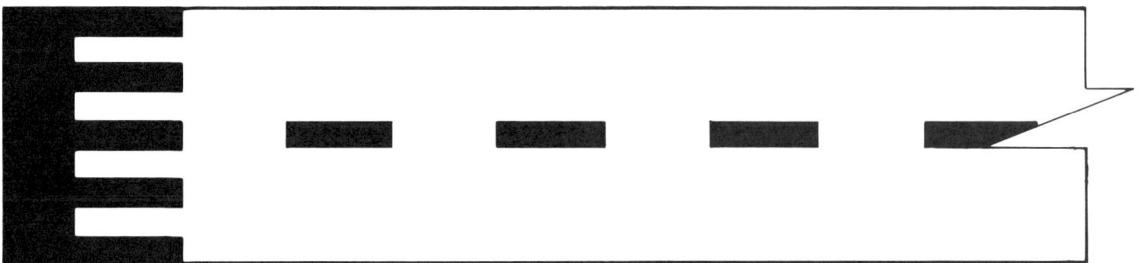

In drawing perspective views you may find the perspective grid on the following page helpful.

If you place a piece of plain paper over the grid below, it will help you to draw basic perspective rectangles which can be used for drawing freehand objects in perspective.

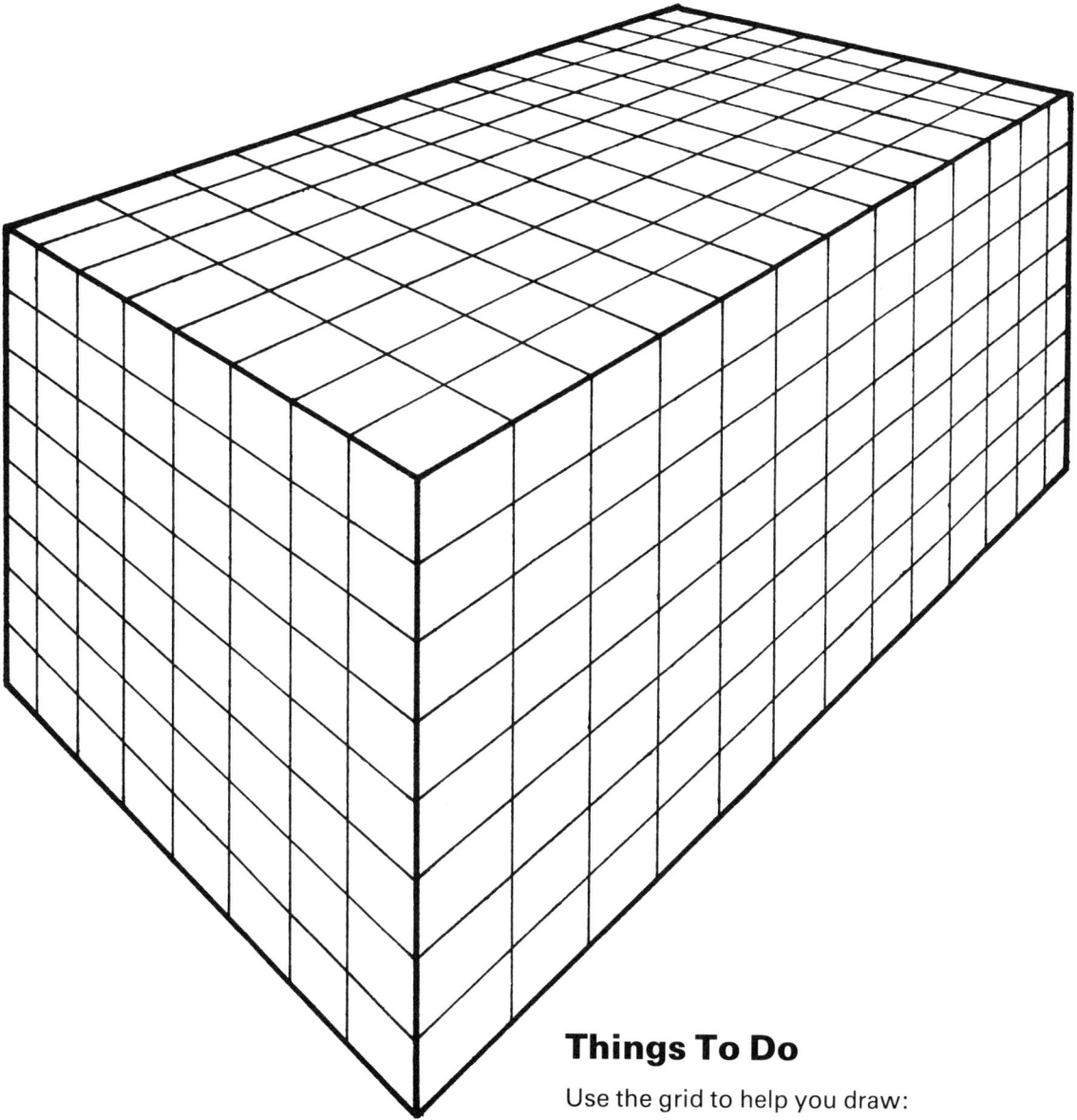

Things To Do

Use the grid to help you draw:

1. A fish tank

2. A bathroom cabinet

3. An electric cooker

4. A coffee table

Isometric Views

Isometric views are similar in some respects to perspective views, but have the advantage of being easy to dimension. Strictly speaking, they do not give a realistic view of an object because no vanishing points are involved. However, isometric views are suitable as workshop diagrams.

When drawing an isometric view we must keep in mind two basic rules:

1. All vertical edges are drawn as vertical lines.

2. All horizontal edges are drawn at 30° to the horizontal (**HP**) as shown below.

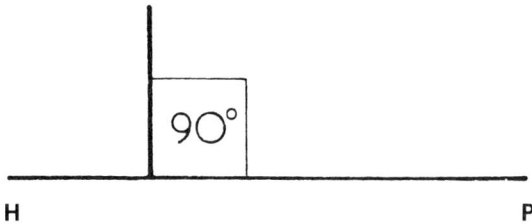

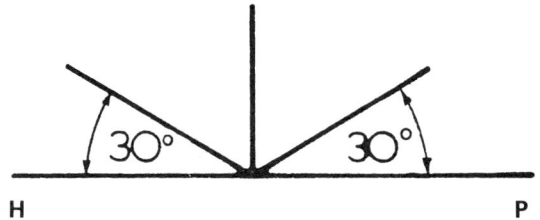

How to draw an Isometric View

1. Draw the leading edge and base lines, as shown below.

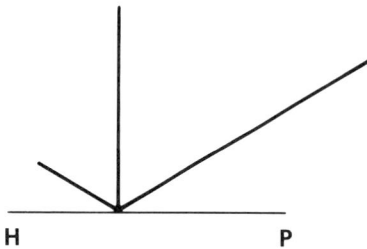

2. Add the front view.

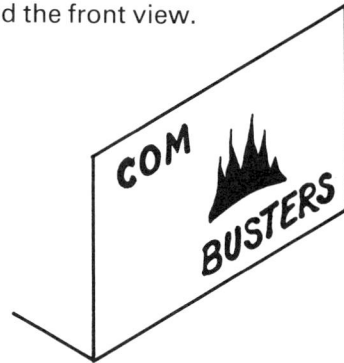

3. Draw the end view.

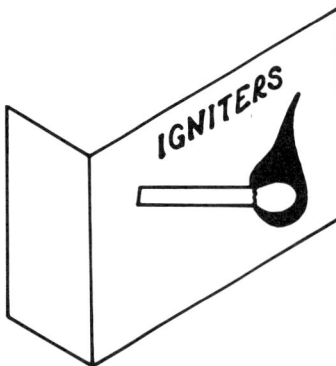

4. Complete the outline.

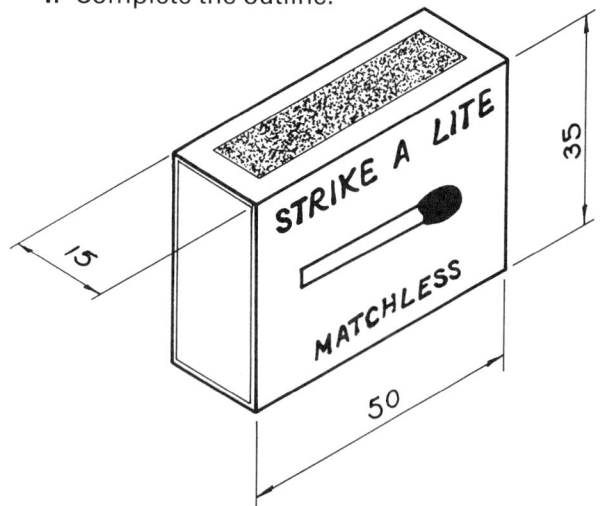

Things To Do

1. Below are shown the front and end elevations of a video cassette. Redraw this cassette as an isometric view and include the main dimensions on your drawing. Opposite is a partial view to help you.

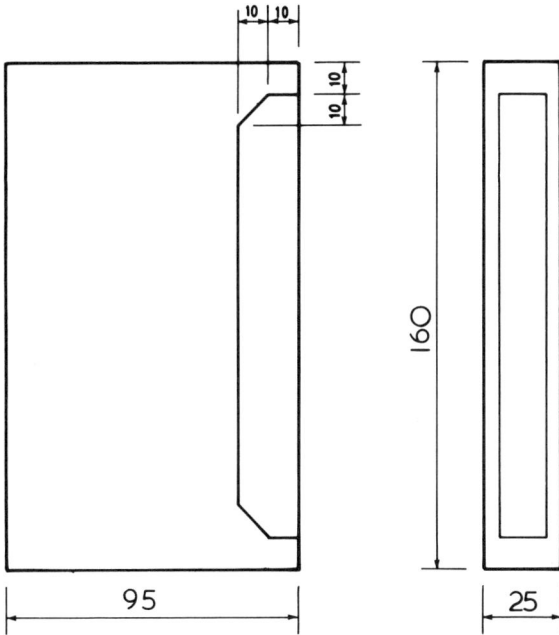

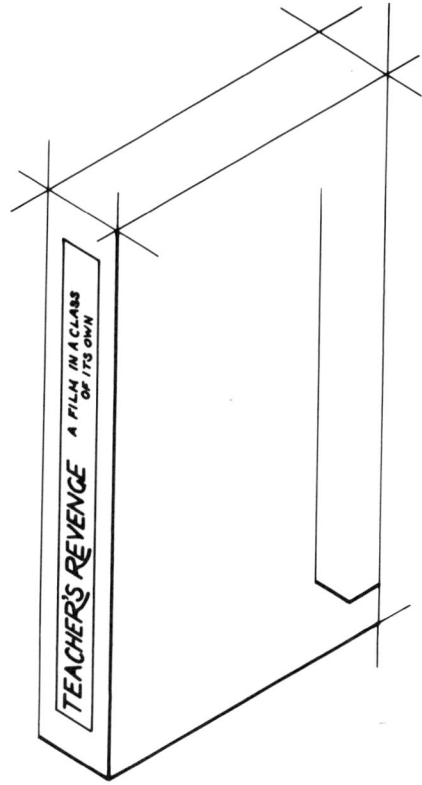

10 | 10

10 | 10

160

95

25

TEACHER'S REVENGE   A FILM IN A CLASS OF ITS OWN

2. The front and end elevations of the robot's body from page 33 are shown here. Redraw this as an isometric view to produce a workshop drawing that would be helpful when making it in the school workshop. You may like to include a design for the robot's chest.

In the next chapter you will see that the front and end elevations of an object shown in this way is called a **two view orthographic projection**.

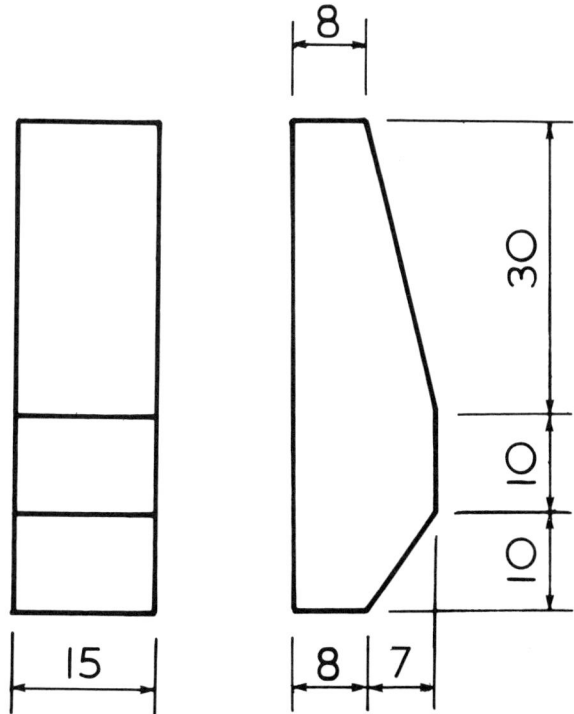

8

30

10

10

15

8 | 7

7 Orthographic projection

Study the drawings below very carefully.

As well as looking at the plan of something, the view seen from arrow **Z**, we can also gain valuable information from other viewpoints. The view that usually gives us *most information* is called the **front elevation**.

The front elevation of the caravan below would be the view seen from arrow **X**. The view seen from arrow **Y** is called the **end elevation**.

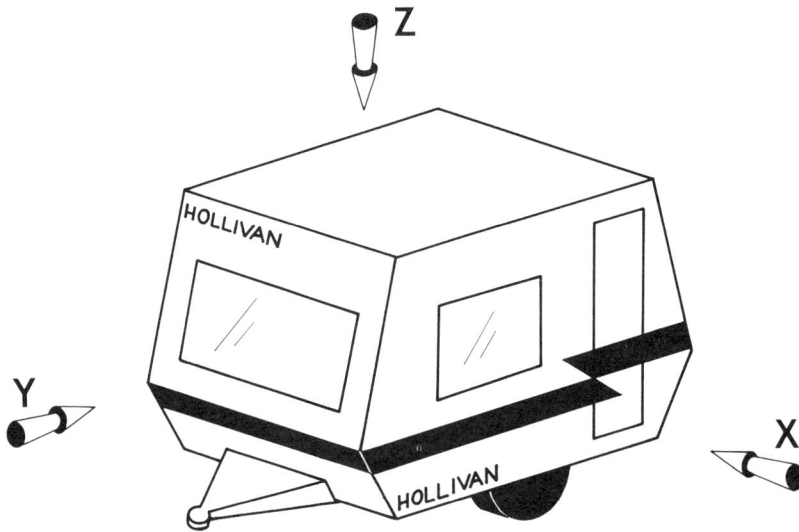

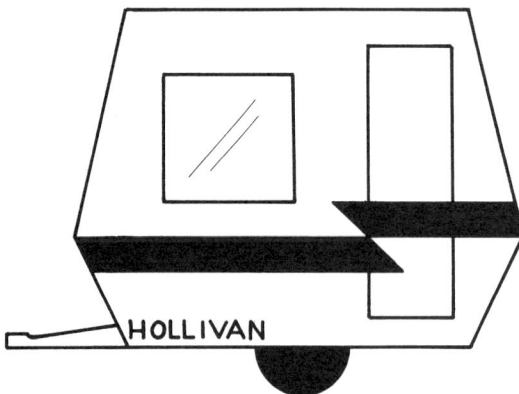

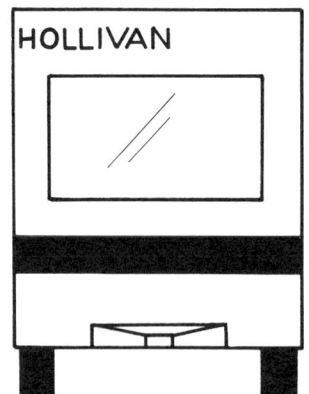

Front elevation

End elevation

Below are the front and end elevations of the Hollivan from the previous page, in outline only.

Notice how the end elevation is *projected* from the front elevation by feint projection lines. This is called a **two view orthographic projection**.

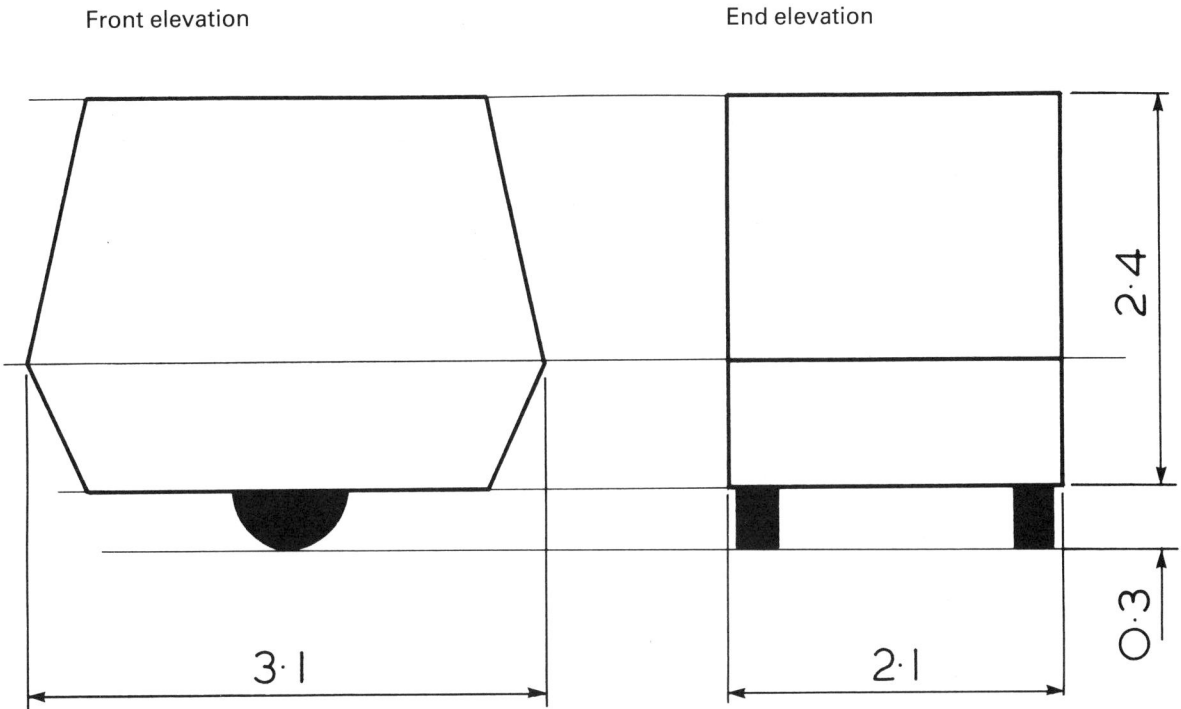

Front elevation

End elevation

The overall dimensions of the Hollivan's door and windows are given opposite.

Things To Do

1. Draw the front and end elevations of the Hollivan above, and position the door and windows where you think best. Your drawing should be to a scale of 1:25. Estimate any dimensions not given.

2. Draw several front elevations of the Hollivan. Colour these drawings to produce attractive colour schemes suitable for a touring caravan.

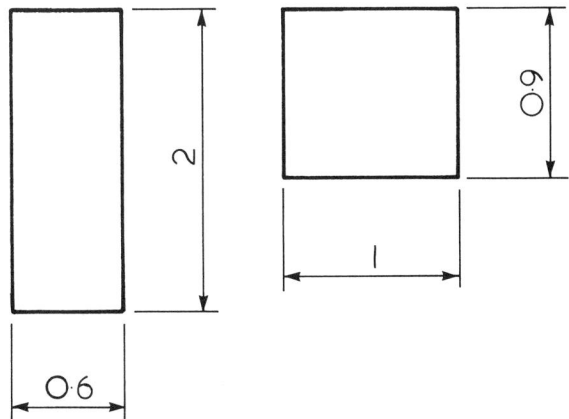

Dimensions in metres

On this page are two further examples of objects drawn in **two view orthographic projection** i.e. combining front and end elevations.

The two items below are *not* drawn to the same scale. All dimensions are in millimetres. Make your own estimate of the dimensions not given.

A

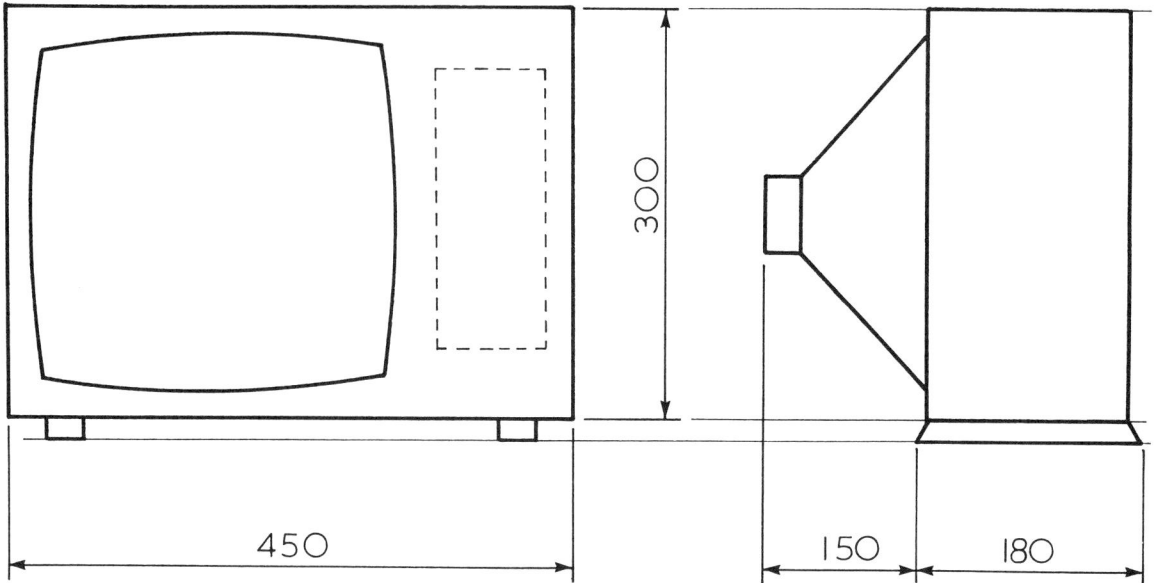

300

450

150

180

B

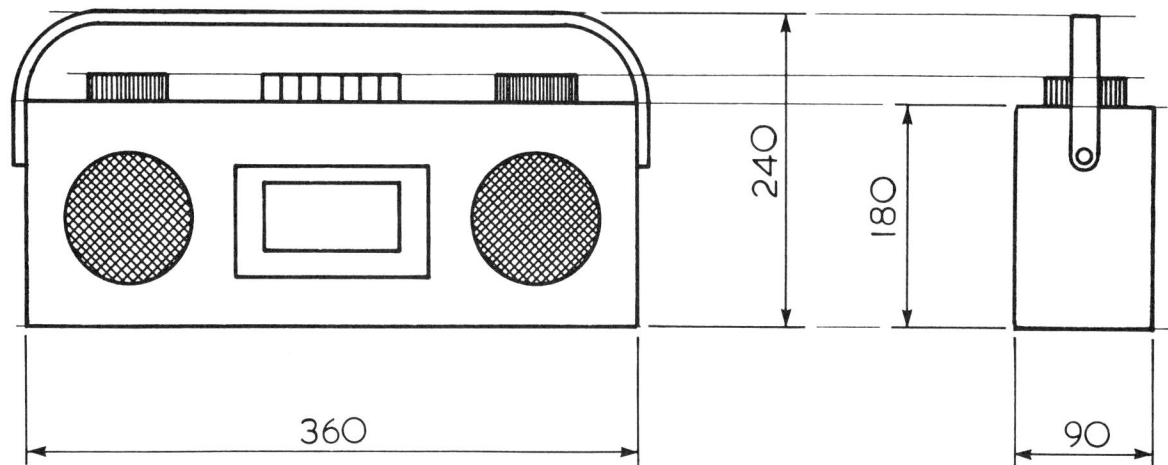

240

180

360

90

Things To Do

1. Drawing **A** above, shows a TV set. Copy the elevations shown to a scale of 1:5. Within the broken lines design a control panel for BBC 1 and 2, ITV and Channel 4. Also include switches for on-off, volume, brightness and contrast.

2. Draw **B** above, to a scale of 1:3. Design a symbol that will indicate the direction in which the tape is played. Include this in your front elevation.

This page shows a model robot made by pupils in the school workshop. Again, this has been drawn in two view orthographic projection with only the major dimensions shown. Make your own estimate for those not given.

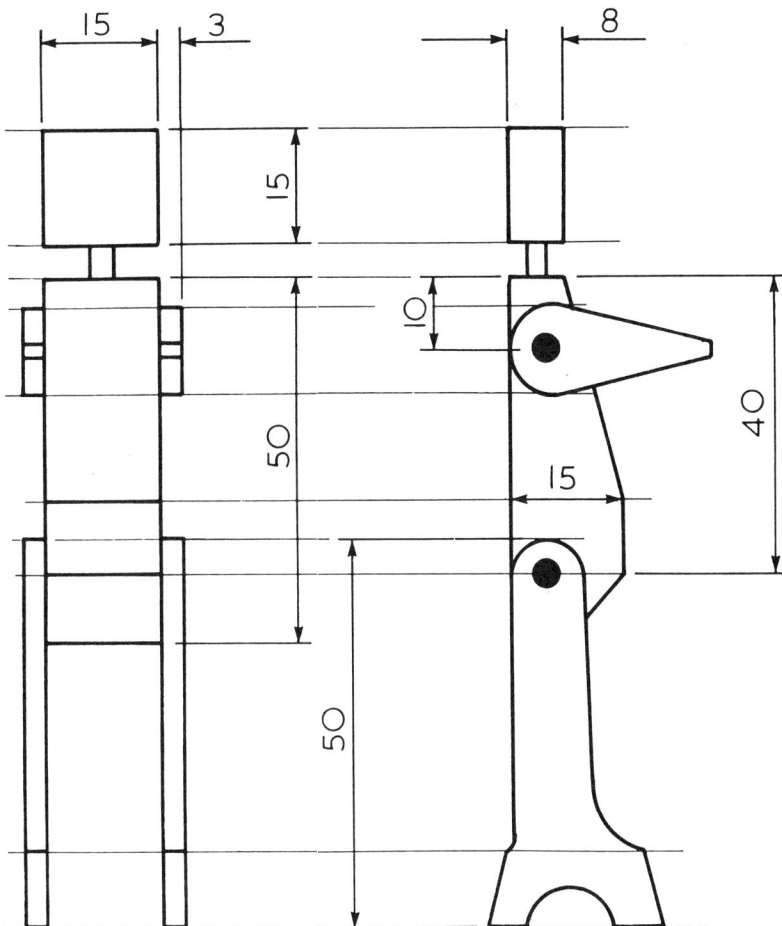

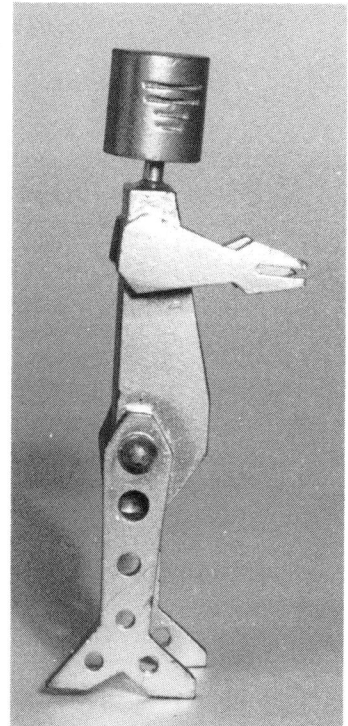

Scale – full-size

Things To Do

1. Draw the elevation of 'Robbie the Robot' above, but design your own 'face' and pattern for the chest. Remember it should be possible to make your designs with the equipment available in school workshops.

2. Within the given dimensions draw Robbie's sister. Design different arms and legs.

If we combine a front elevation, end elevation and plan in one drawing, as below, this will help us to see what the object will look like. This is called a **three view orthographic projection**. These drawings are often dimensioned so we can see the finished sizes of the object.

Such drawings are therefore very useful when making something in the workshop.

Notice how the plan of the Hollivan is projected directly below the front elevation. This is called **first angle orthographic projection**.

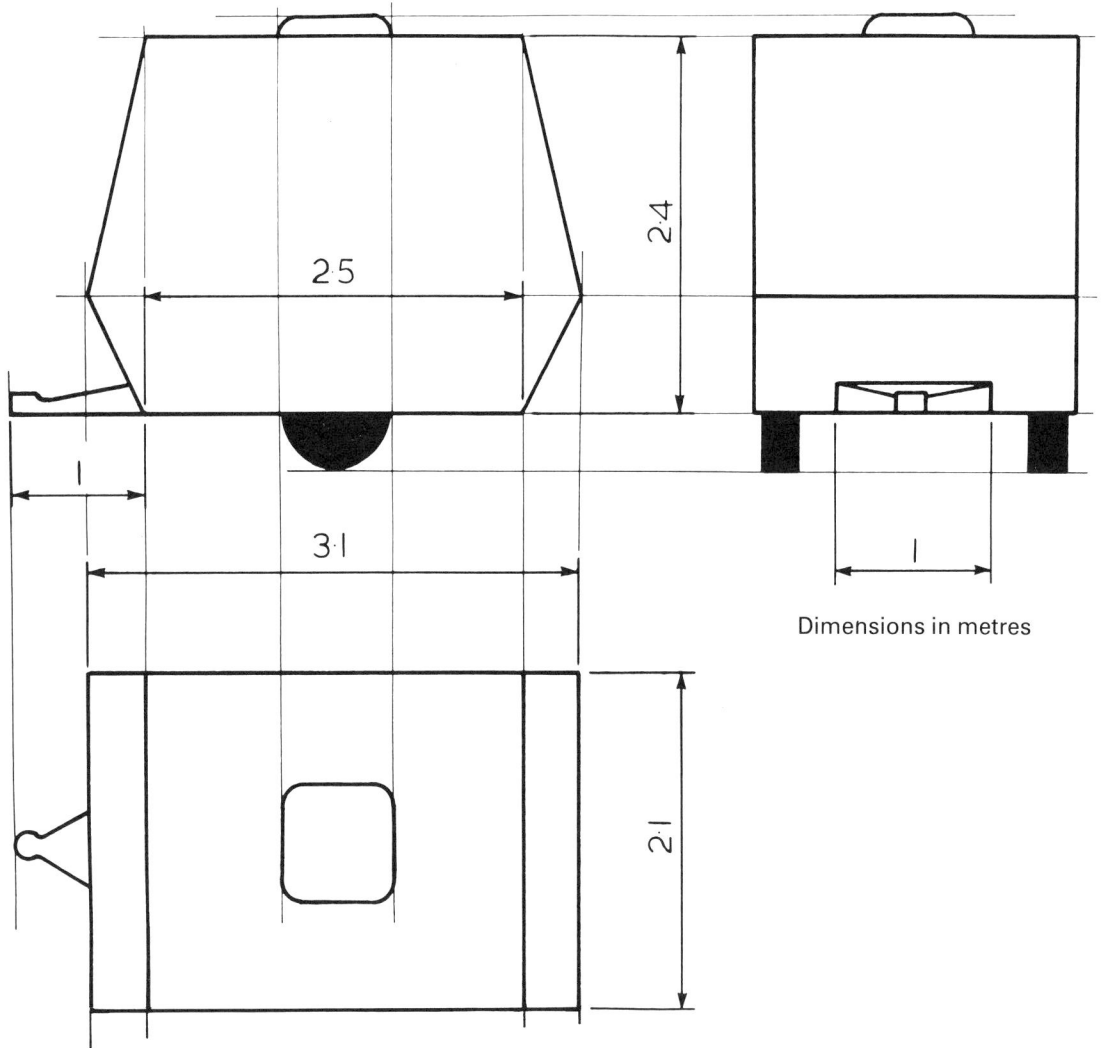

2·5

2·4

3·1

1

2·1

1

Dimensions in metres

Things To Do

1. Complete the drawing above by positioning a door and windows, where you think they should be, onto the three elevations.

2. Draw a front elevation of the Hollivan hitched to a car (perhaps the car on page 18).

3. Many large caravans can be found fixed to a site, especially at the seaside. Design and draw to a suitable scale such a caravan in three view orthographic projection. The caravan is 12 metres long, 2.5 metres wide and 2.7 metres high (including the wheels). Show the position of all doors and windows. Colour your drawing.

The photograph shows a model racing car that has been made in the school workshop. The working drawing (in three view orthographic projection) shown below is incomplete – all three elevations have something missing.

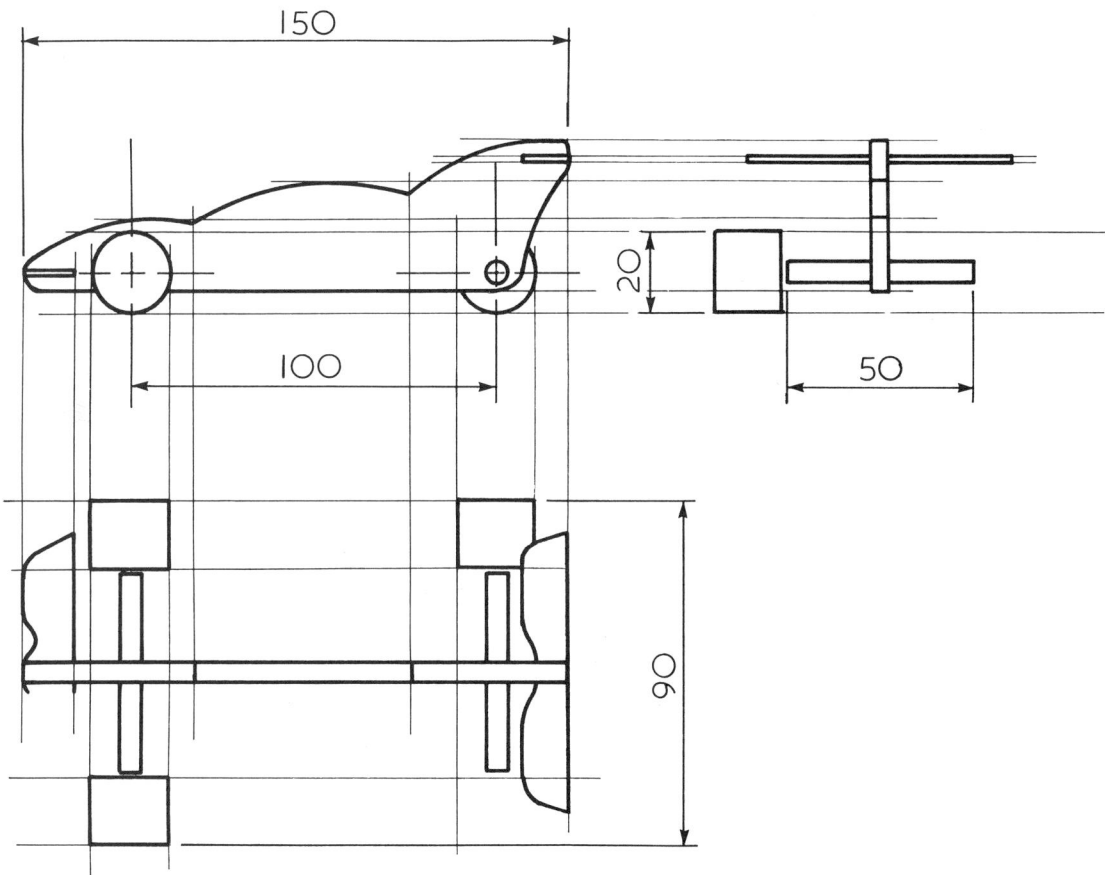

Things To Do

1. Complete the workshop drawing above. Estimate any dimensions that are not shown.

2. Using the same wheel positions design and draw an alternative body shape for the racing car. Colour your drawing.

Here is a wooden model of a space shuttle.

Below is a three view orthographic workshop drawing of this model. The front and end elevations are drawn complete and include the major sizes.

Can you guess which elevation is shown here only partially completed?

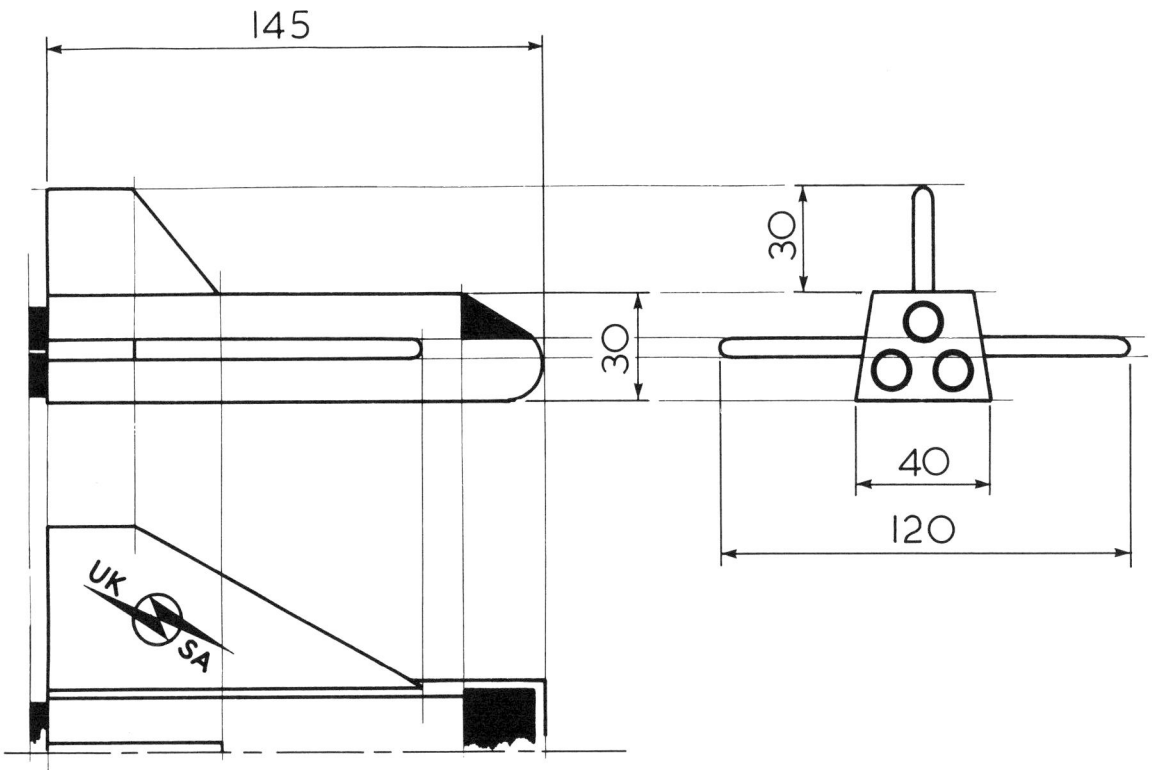

Things To Do

1. Design a symbol for use on this shuttle which belongs to the United Kingdom Space Agency (UKSA).

2. Copy the front and end elevations above but draw them full-size. Any dimensions not given are left up to you.

3. Using all the information on this page complete a workshop drawing of the shuttle which includes a plan view. (You can add your symbol design onto the wing if you wish.)

8 Developments

Developments are useful when an article is to
be made from sheet material e.g. metal, acrylic
sheet or paper. They give us the shape of the
material before it is bent, folded or cut.

The object drawn below is an ordinary
envelope. When we draw an article opened
out in this way we call it a **development**.

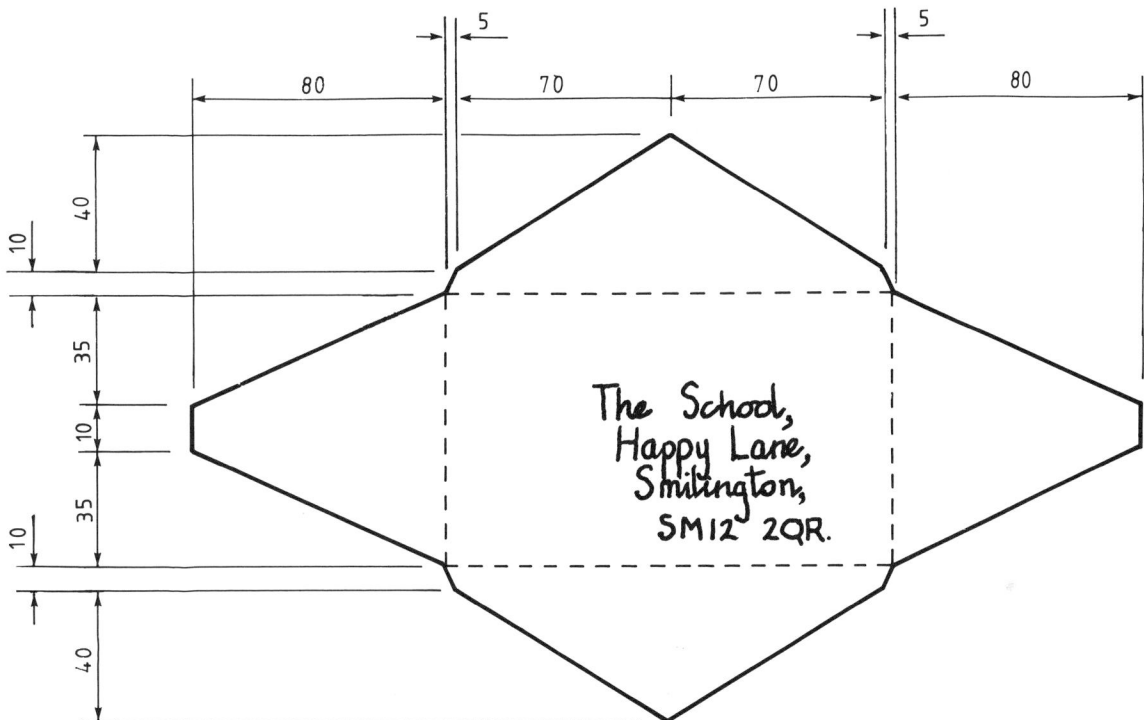

The School,
Happy Lane,
Smilington,
SM12 2QR.

Things To Do

1. A birthday card measures 180 × 180 mm.
Design an envelope which could be used to
send the card through the post. Cut out
your design and fold it to test that it is
suitable.

2. A special envelope is required for disco
tickets. Each ticket measures 100 × 70 mm
and will not be sent through the post.
Design a suitable envelope and a symbol
which could be printed on the envelope.

On the right is a photograph of a tray made in the school workshop from a single piece of acrylic sheet. Before it was made a development of the tray's basic shape was made as shown below.

The broken lines show where the acrylic sheet is to be bent. The shaded areas show the sides and handles.

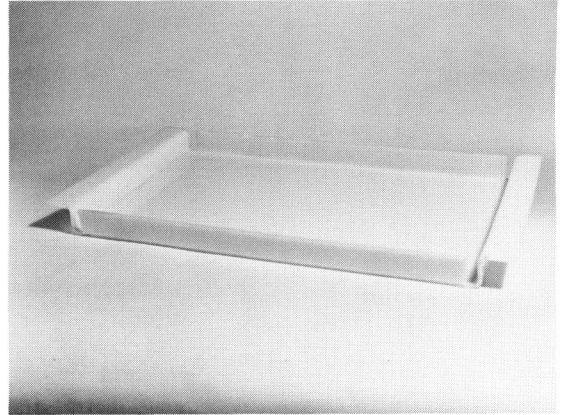

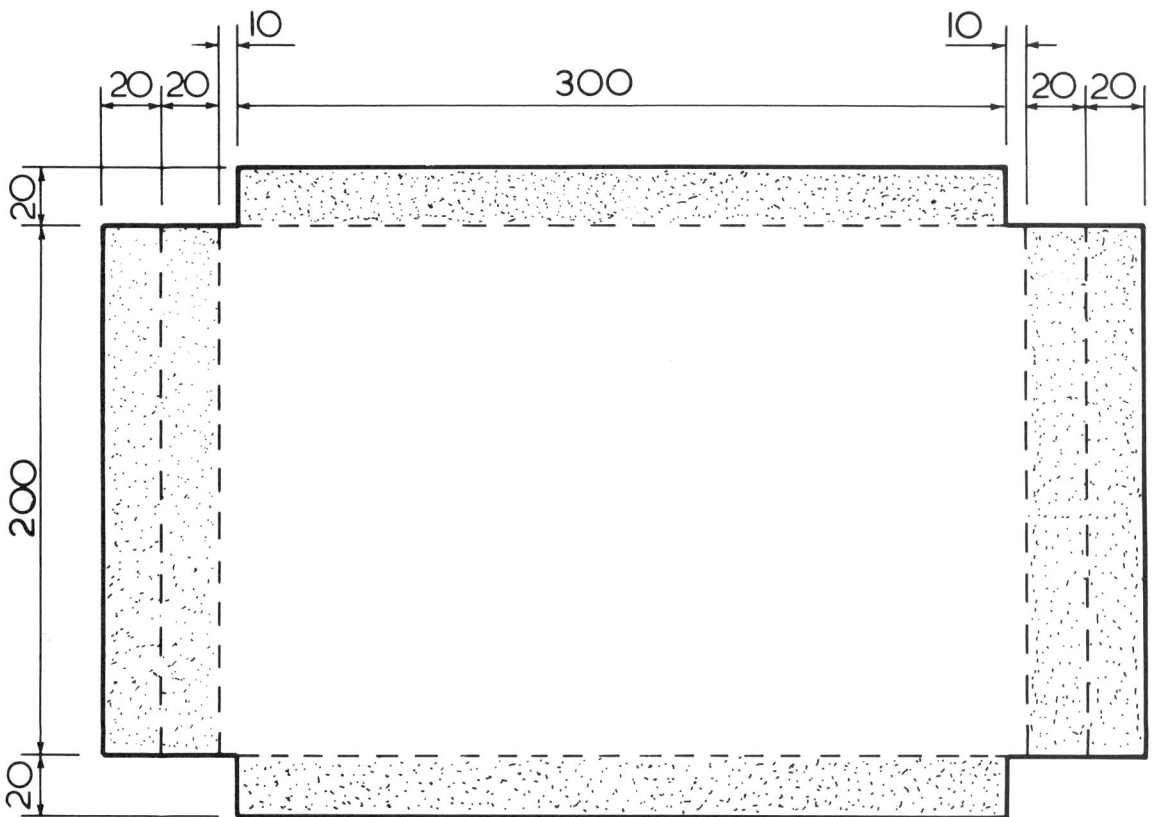

Things To Do

1. Draw the above development but design your own handles and sides. Produce three different designs.

2. Make a card model of your favourite design.

As cassette players and video recorders have become more popular the problem arises of how to store the cassettes. A basic concept for a rack to solve this problem is shown here.

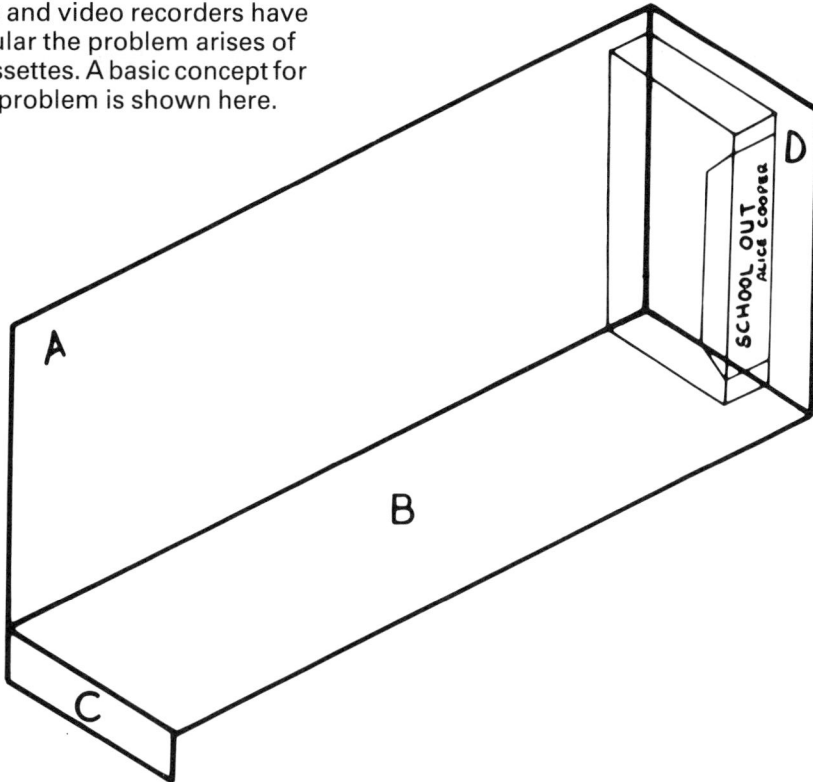

Below is the development of such a design as it would be laid out on a piece of Perspex, for making in a school workshop.

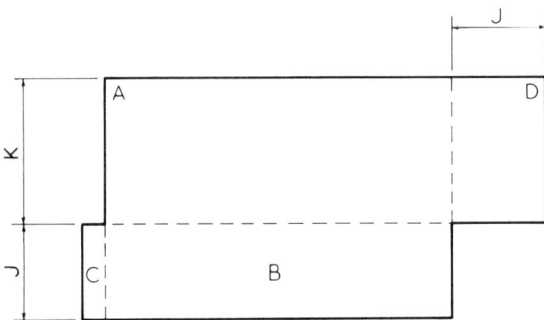

The broken lines show where the material will be folded.

The sizes for BETA video tape cassettes are 157 × 95 × 25 mm and the VHS are 190 × 105 × 25 mm.

Things To Do

1. Find out the main sizes **J** and **K** for storing either Beta or VHS cassettes on the above development.

2. Using the basic development above, design different shapes for parts **A** and **D**.

3. Draw a development of your design full-size on card using the sizes you found out in your research. Cut out your design, fold it into shape and see if it is suitable.

9 Design your own craftwork

The design method on the following pages will help you when designing items to be made in the school workshop. Each stage in the design method is indicated at the top of the following pages.

Poor design

When you are given a project to design, keep your ideas simple. Very often we look for complications which do not exist. The best ideas are usually straightforward solutions to a problem. If you look at the the two shapes opposite, which are designs for an acrylic key fob, you will see that the simple shape is more pleasing to look at and will do the job better than the complicated shape.

Below is a flow chart which will help you think in a logical way when working on design problems. Look at the flow chart very carefully. Then design your own flow chart (with the same number of stages), using the information given below.

Good design

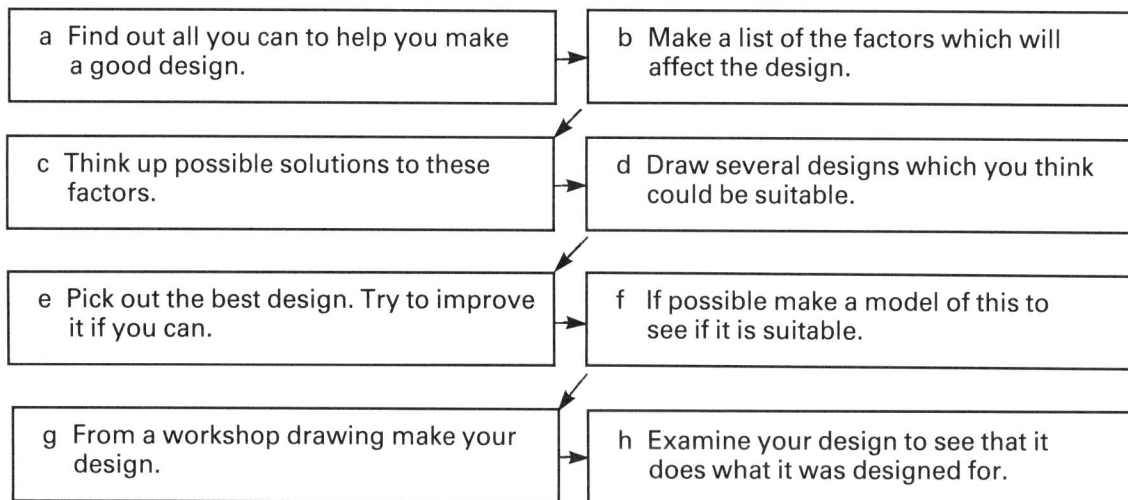

a Find out all you can to help you make a good design.

b Make a list of the factors which will affect the design.

c Think up possible solutions to these factors.

d Draw several designs which you think could be suitable.

e Pick out the best design. Try to improve it if you can.

f If possible make a model of this to see if it is suitable.

g From a workshop drawing make your design.

h Examine your design to see that it does what it was designed for.

REMEMBER! KEEP YOUR IDEAS SIMPLE

Design Method — Parts a and b

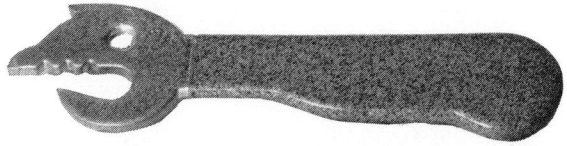

On the right is a photograph of a novelty bottle-opener made in a school workshop. We are going to use this example to illustrate this particular design method.

Below is the layout of a sheet which is called a design brief. Each time you are set a design problem, you should complete a sheet such as this. It will help you think carefully about the problem and give you a better chance of producing a good design.

This design brief is for a novelty bottle-opener which has the face of a monster. The shape of the mouth has been decided for you, see page 43.

1. Draw up the design brief and complete it by listing other factors which will affect the design, in the box labelled Design Considerations and Limitations. The first three have been done for you.

DESIGN BRIEF

TO _design and make a novelty bottle-opener which has the face of a monster._

The following conditions apply

Materials Available

1 off B.D.M.S. 40 x 3 x 165.
Dip coating plastic – various colours.

Tools Available

A full range of workshop hand tools.
Pillar drilling machine.

Design Considerations and Limitations

1. Your design must include the mouth shape as given.
2. The mouth must rotate to remove the bottle top.
3. A handle will be needed to provide the leverage.
4.
5.
6.

NAME I. B. Thirsty   DATE 1st Oct.

Form 2 / R.

41

Design Method – Part c

Below you can see the stages in developing one possible design for the bottle-opener taking into account the information from the design brief on the previous page. In the same way, using your own ideas, your design will be developed.

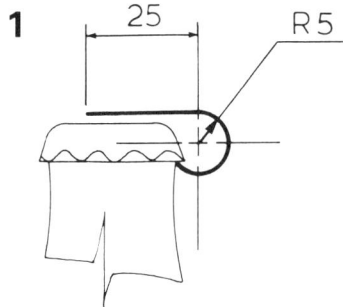

1

Your design must include the mouth shape as given.

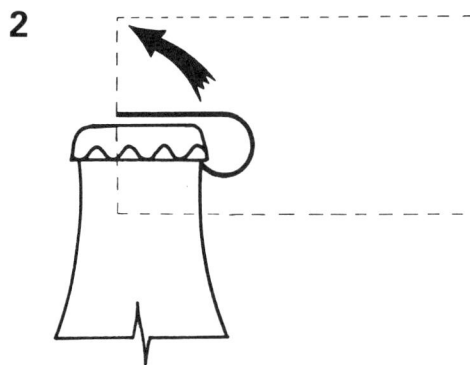

2

The mouth must rotate to remove the bottle top.

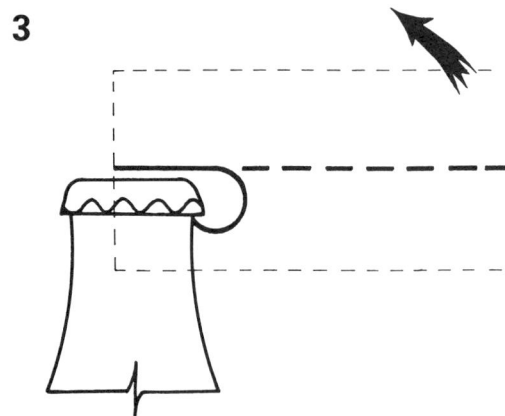

3

A handle will be needed to provide the leverage.

4

A monster's face must be included.

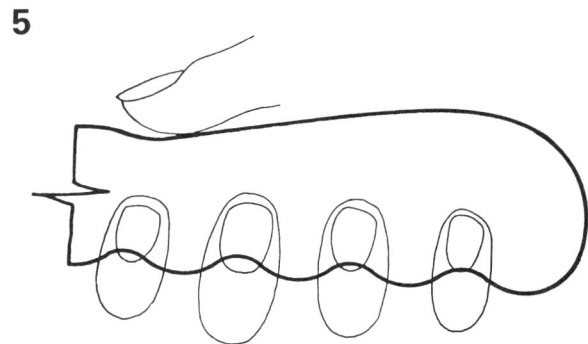

5

The handle must be comfortable to grip.

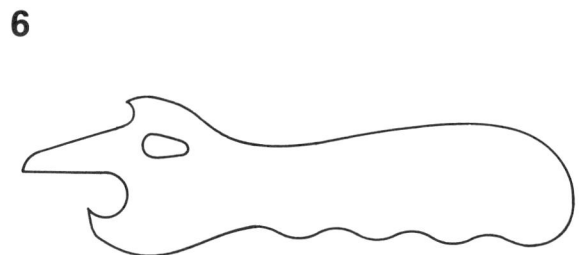

6

There should be no sharp edges on the handle.

Once you have some ideas for a design, you need to consider how good they are and how they could be improved.

Design Method — Parts d and e

You may have to produce a number of designs before you have one which is suitable.

Notice that the shape of the mouth is always the same.

The dimensions below show the maximum size of the head.

1. Complete six alternative designs for the head of your bottle-opener.

2. Choose your best design and draw it full-size on a separate sheet.

The presentation of your work will be improved by the sensible use of colour.

This mouth shape must be included in your designs

25

40

14

DRILL ⌀ 10

NAME I.B. Thirsty   Designs for the head

Design Method — Parts d and e

Once the design for the head of the opener has been chosen, the next stage is to design a suitable handle.

Again, you may have to produce many designs and experiment with shapes in plasticine or card before you are satisfied with it.

The dimensions given show the maximum size of the handle.

Remember that the handle must match and fit the chosen design for the head. Again, use colour to improve the appearance of your work.

1. Complete three designs for the handle of your bottle-opener.

2. Choose the design you think most suitable and draw it full-size on a separate sheet.

NAME I. B. Thirsty   Designs for the handle.

Design Method — Parts f and g

Your chosen head and handle designs may now be combined to produce a completed design.

At this stage you may like to produce a full-size card model or mock-up of your design to help you decide if it is suitable. If it is, then a workshop drawing, like the one below, will be needed. Can you think why?

This design could then be made in the school workshop.

Using the method described on the previous pages, carefully produce designs for:

1. A key fob to be made from acrylic sheet such as Perspex.

2. A brass name-plate to be fixed to a school-bag.

3. A set of coasters made from plywood or acrylic sheet.

4. A Perspex paper-knife for opening letters.

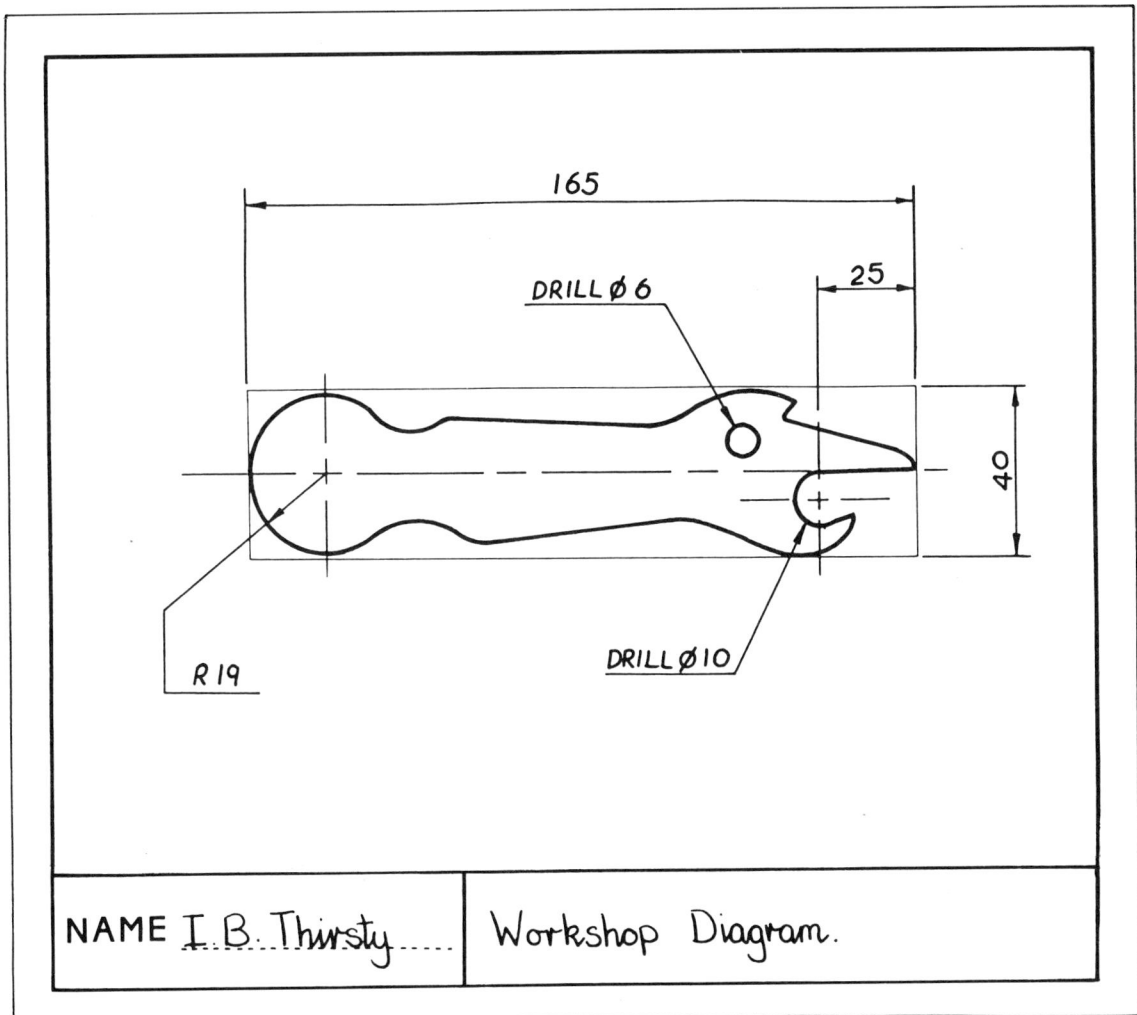

165

DRILL ∅ 6

25

40

R 19

DRILL ∅ 10

NAME I. B. Thirsty   Workshop Diagram.

Design Method – Part h

When you have finished designing and making a particular assignment, you need to decide how well your design solved the original problem, and how it could be improved. This process is called **appraisal**.

You can use the information on your chart to help you write an assessment or criticism of your work.

Below is an **appraisal chart** to help you.

1. Draw your own chart and tick the appropriate box but remember not all the items listed below will be needed for every project. For different design problems, different items may have to be added to the list.

	YES	NO	COMMENT
Does your finished article do the job it was designed for?			
Is it safe to use?			
Is it comfortable to use?			
Is the shape pleasing to look at?			
Does the colour suit the finished article?			
Do the colour and texture suit its surroundings?			
Can you use it without regular adjustment or unnecessary servicing?			

10 Design assignments

Using the method outlined in the previous chapter, make designs for the following items. A few design considerations are included to help you; perhaps you can think of some more.

1. A support is required to hold the commercially made thermometer shown opposite.

Design Considerations

(a) Free standing or wall mounted?
(b) The thermometer should be easily visible.
(c)

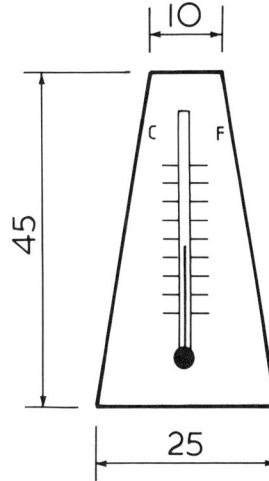

2. Design a trophy plaque to display the small medal and inscription plate shown opposite.

Design Considerations

(a) What is the most suitable shape to hold the medal and inscription plate?
(b)

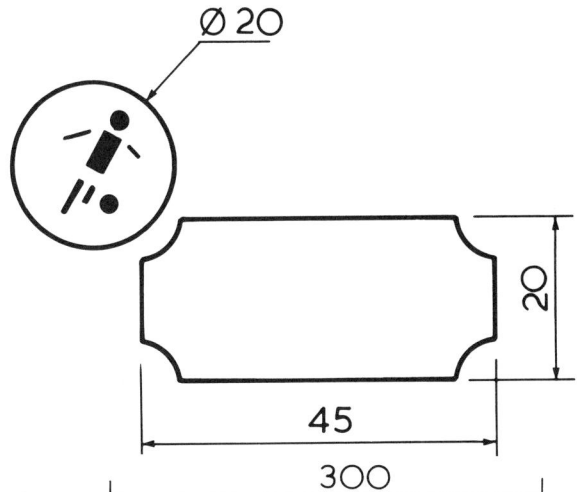

3. A marble game, the object of which is to move a marble from **A** to **B** avoiding at least 6 obstacles.

Design Considerations

(a) The game should require skill to play.
(b) Each obstacle should present a fresh challenge.
(c)

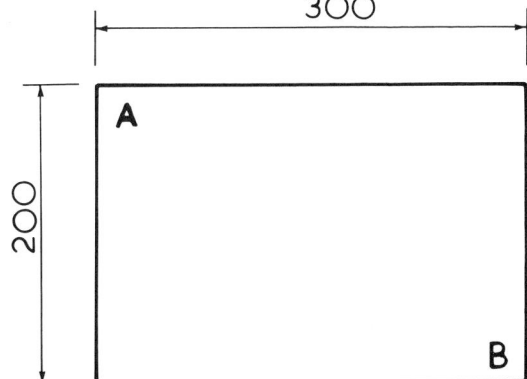

47

4. A storage system is needed to hold six of the coasters (drink mats) shown opposite.

Design Considerations

(a) The coasters should be easy to remove and replace.

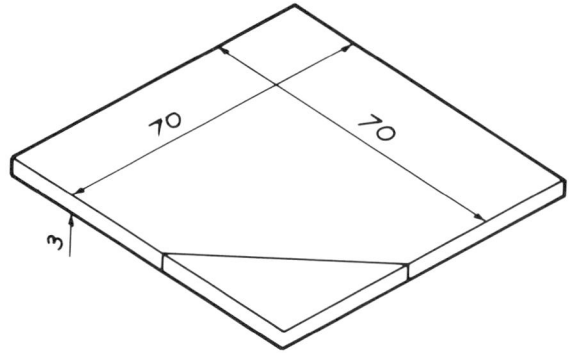

(b)

70 70 3

5. A holder is required for the candle shown opposite.

Design Considerations

(a) The holder should be stable.
(b) The molten wax should be caught.
(c)

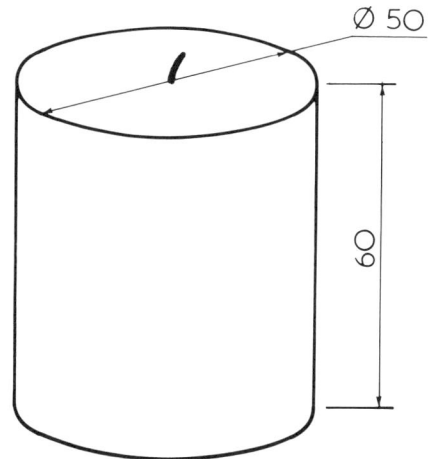

Ø 50

60

6. Shown opposite, and drawn actual-size so you can measure them, are two special edition postage stamps. In the complete set there are three large and four small stamps. Design a cabinet to hold this set of commemorative stamps.

Design Considerations

(a) All the stamps should be displayed.

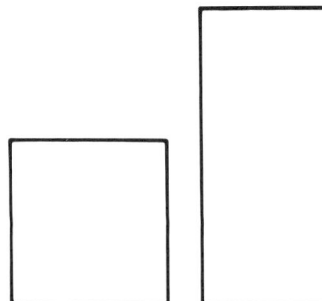

(b)